SEMIOTEXT(E) NATIVE AGENTS SERIES

© 2009 by Semiotext(e) and Jean-Luc Hennig

Published by Semiotext(e)
2007 Wilshire Blvd., Suite 427, Los Angeles, CA 90057
www.semiotexte.com

Special thanks to John Ebert, Marcelle Robin, Igor Schimek, and Alice Tassel.

All photos of Grisélidis Réal courtesy of Igor Schimek. All rights reserved.
Back cover photo: Jean-Luc Hennig and Grisélidis Réal in the 1970s.

Design by Hedi El Kholti

ISBN: 978-1-58435-078-1
Distributed by The MIT Press, Cambridge, Mass. and London, England
Printed in the United States of America

THE LITTLE BLACK BOOK

OF GRISÉLIDIS RÉAL

DAYS AND NIGHTS OF AN ANARCHIST WHORE

Jean-Luc Hennig

Translated by Ariana Reines

Contents

Grisélidis Réal with Barbara, Marylou and unknown at the Aiglon in Geneva in the mid-'80s.

Ariana Reines

Translator's Note

This book was first published in 1981, when Grisélidis Réal was in her fifties. By that time, Réal was a well-known public figure in Europe. She had published two autobiographical books, *Le noir est une couleur* (*Black is a Color*) and *Carnet de bal d'une courtisane* (*Dance Card of a Courtesan*), and her stories, poems, and political writings had been appearing in newspapers and reviews for at least a decade.

Born in Lausanne in 1929, Grisélidis moved at age 6 to Alexandria, Egypt, where her father was a school principal, and then to Athens, Greece, where he died when she was 9. After a rigid upbringing by her mother, Grisélidis studied industrial art in Zurich, obtaining a diploma in 1949 that she would eventually describe as "useless." She married at 20, had a son in 1952, separated from her husband, and in 1955 gave birth to a daughter, by another man. Through an attempted reunion with her estranged husband, a second son was born, in 1956, followed by divorce. Her fourth child, a son, was born in 1959. It must have been around this time that, through the course of a treatment for tuberculosis in an Alpine sanitarium, broke and depressed, Grisélidis turned her first trick. She soon went to Munich with a lover and two of her children, and began to work in earnest as a prostitute, selling marijuana on the side. While imprisoned for six months and three weeks for selling drugs, Réal began to paint and write. Upon her release, she attempted to quit prostitution, having decided to devote herself to art and literature. It was during this time that she wrote *Le noir est une couleur*, which was published in 1974, and which, along with all of her other books, including posthumous volumes of poetry, remains in print in French. Her sex work hiatus lasted seven years; by the middle of the seventies she was participating in political actions, in particular the "Prostitutes' Revolution" in Paris, in which five hundred female prostitutes occupied a church, La Chapelle Saint-Bernard, asserting that prostitution was a choice, and rejecting the idea that a woman would only prostitute herself if compelled or coerced by a pimp. In 1977, she returned to Switzerland, where, in Geneva, she would continue to work as an active prostitute until the age of 66. In 1982, she was among the founders of the sex-workers' rights organization Aspasie. From her small apartment in the red-light district, she set about creating an international center for research and documentation concerning prostitution.

It seems worth noting, for American and English-speaking readers, that prostitution has been legal in Switzerland since 1942, that, as of today, Swiss prostitutes pay VAT (Value Added Tax) on their services, and that some even accept credit cards. Shifting transit and residency laws in the EU mean that most prostitutes in Switzerland are foreigners, from South America, France, Eastern Europe, and the Middle East. Les Pâquis, the red-light neighborhood where Grisélidis Réal lived for most of her life, whose crime and noise she vividly describes, is still full of whores, and, as of 2006, was a 2.65 billion dollar industry. Because prostitution was legal during Grisélidis Réal's life, her activism centered on responding to moralizers whose condemnation of sex work was both paternalist and misogynist, and to feminists who considered sex work to be exploitative or emblematic of patriarchal repression. Réal's work as a writer and public figure not only helped to tone down whatever lurid sensationalism attended the public's idea of what prostitutes actually do, or who johns are, but it also revealed the insight and mastery required to do the job well—a menu of skills and abilities closely related to what makes a good psychotherapist, for example, or effective leaders.

> It's time for all the men who come to us "weary and burdened" as it says in the Bible—those we save from suicide and solitude, those who find in our arms and in our vaginas the vital force that's only thwarted elsewhere, those we send away with their balls light and sunshine in their hearts—to stop hassling us, judging us, disowning us, taxing us, beating us, locking us up, taking our kids to put them on Public Assistance, locking up our lovers and boyfriends…[1]

And yet this book does more than document prostitution's legitimacy as a profession. There's an important intersection between the—often fictional—divulgence of the particular wisdom and secrets of women of pleasure (Cleland's *Fanny Hill*, Colette's *Chéri*) and the profoundly sexualized idea of a woman, not necessarily a whore, talking candidly about what she feels, who she is, what she *knows*—Chaucer's Wife of Bath, The Book of Margery Kempe, Diderot's *Les Bijoux Indiscrets*, *The Story of Mary Maclane*, the 1st-person narratives of Semiotext(e)'s Native Agents series. This book, though its contents are para-literary, (interviews and an annotated client list), is conducted by two people of letters—Hennig, the writer and sociologist, and Réal, the well-read writer and activist whore. Yeah, it's a sociological document, but imbued with tropes from literature and the occasional purplish flourish. I think Réal's

---

1. Réal, Grisélidis. *Carnet de bal d'une courtisane*. Verticales, Paris: 2005.

descriptions of assholes are among the most exquisite, and efficient, ever written.

This text presented several difficulties for translation, and I want to note them. First of all, the woman speaking is in her fifties, talking to a dear friend in the eighties, in Geneva, having worked as a prostitute on and off for twenty-odd years. Her diction is a combination of sometimes antiquated, but on the whole familiar fuck slang, racial frankness, gentility, and Swiss (not Parisian, though that's there too) idioms. I wanted to bring her rhythm and tone across without deforming the peculiar, delightful combination of propriety and obscenity with which she describes things. A few words presented particular difficulty.

Enculer means to fuck in the ass, to assfuck, to bugger, (as Britons used to say, apparently), or, to use a more contemporary American term, to ream. Grisélidis uses the verb frequently in the *Little Black Book*, to indicate something she does to a client—though I think the verb has a broad application for her. At first I thought that the frequency of the verb indicated that she mounted and rode her clients, fucking them with some kind of strap-on. But prostheses like that only show up twice in the book. There is one direct reference to a vibrator (*un vibro-masseur*), followed by an exclamation point, suggesting some kind of novelty or squeamish delight associated with the device. At another point she mentions a "big plastic electric cock." For a sex worker to refer to a vibrator or dildo in this way suggests that she does not often use tools of this kind. Whether this has to do with the progress of the sex toy industry or Grisélidis's age or some other matter, I don't know. In any case, it means that *enculer* for Grisélidis does not denote "full-on" anal sex.

Even though "assfuck" might suggest heavier penetration, I've decided to use the word as it functions within Grisélidis's usage: in her little black book, *enculer* means a finger or two or three in the ass. Because at times she simply writes *enculer*, whereas other times she makes specific mention of her finger or fingers, as in, "So I put a finger in his ass with Vaseline, and then I feel his prostate hardening…" I take *enculer* to indicate, for our purposes here, manual penetration of the anus that does not require the same delicacy and care as instances in which she mentions the finger, the hand.

Through the course of this book, Grisélidis talks about fucking Turks, Moroccans, Algerians, Spaniards, Italians, Portuguese, Black Africans, Black Americans, and some French and Swiss men as well. French has a blunt way of nominalizing people and persons according to their age or race or profession or situation. For example, an old man is simply a "vieillard"—this emphasizes the old (vieil) while underplaying the human. Racial difference and racially-inflected desire are totally open, specific, canny, and expressly subjective in Grisélidis's descriptions. She has a history of falling for, and rhapsodizing over, black men, especially black Americans. I went with translating the French word *nègres* the way they translate Genet—as "blacks" and not "black men" much less "negroes," which would have been overly archaic. I'm not going to gloss over, explain, apologize for, promote, or become the exegete of, Grisélidis's racial stuff. She's not an idiot; she has no need to homogenize the world. If her longing for difference sometimes verges on exoticism or orientalism, well then, it does.

The reader might be astonished by Grisélidis's relationship to condoms, which she rarely uses. Her assertion that using condoms wasn't necessarily the best, or only, way to avoid HIV infection caused controversy in Europe. In a 2005 interview on Swiss television, she said:

There was a time when we almost never used condoms. But AIDS had not been discovered. I never said that people should not wear condoms. What I said was that health, true health, is not to be found in a plastic [*sic*] condom. There are people who ruin their immune systems in other ways. By abusing chemicals and drugs, for example. Tranquilizers, alcohol abuse, cigarettes, sleeping pills, amphetamines, drugs. All this contributes to the ruin of your immune system. A condom's not always enough by itself—though I never said people shouldn't wear them. I did not often use them, but, unfortunately for science, I don't have AIDS. I've recently been tested, and I still don't have it. There's a risk that you run, certainly.

In a much earlier interview for a Swiss television show called "La vie littéraire," or "The Literary Life," which aired in December of 1970, Grisélidis discusses her writing, her experience in jail, her love of black men, her rejection of what she calls Genevan "frigidity" and Europe's "degenerate" view of eroticism. The journalist, Frank Jotterand, notices that Grisélidis owns many books by Henri Michaux. "I admire Michaux enormously," she says. "I admire him above all because of the power of his interior vision, which is linked to primitive art at its most extraordinary and most abstract." The interviewer notes that next to Michaux are books by Henry Miller. Asked what she thinks of him, Grisélidis says:

A: He's the pope of literature! And of life. This is a man who has understood what it is to live. What he writes is what he lives. It is what everyone should live. Women and men and children of every race. Miller understands magic, he understands love, understands women, and he understands spirit, esprit, above all.
Q: *To live like Miller is to live with erotic passion and spiritual passion, altogether.*
A: The spirit is what controls true eroticism, in any case.
Q: *And what is eroticism to you?*

A: It is the sublimation of certain sexual acts—in which sentiment, feeling, plays a part. And a great deal of esprit.

Q: *Do you consider Sade to have been a spiritual master?*

A: Sade was a spiritual master, but, in negative, if you will. It's his genius that saved him. But he must have suffered a great deal, I imagine.

Q: *Why?*

A: Because it's hard to celebrate cruelty. Through acts or in spirit. It's hard. It's not happiness: it's a sacrifice.

On March 9, 2009, the body of Grisélidis Réal was exhumed from the working-class cemetery in Geneva where she had been buried in 2005. Her body was moved, by official resolution, and to the outrage or delight of various Helvetic sensibilities, to Geneva's prestigious Cemetery of Kings, where Jorge Luis Borges is buried, among other writers, and where John Calvin himself is at eternal rest.

Grisélidis Réal in her apartment in 1970. Courtesy of Igor Schimek.

Grisélidis Réal

The Way Blacks Dance

The way blacks dance, the way lions make love, the way wolves howl from hunger, you cry, you open your veins with words. It's stronger than you. The book is a hydra installed in your head; it devours you down to the last drop of blood.

Riveted to it, you stop existing. There are no more hours, no more day, no more night. The only love left to you is a silent hyena devouring your guts. Yes, that's what writing is. To empty yourself down to the marrow, to live another life, to be caught in a text, dragged into it alive. To laugh, cry, burn on words, get flayed on them. Scream for mercy and go back to get stabbed in the neck. Doubt yourself at every word, at every sentence. To give throat to the silence. To know that nothing is ever finished, never established. That you must start over every time, risk your skin at its most intimate every day, lose everything, win everything back.

The book that's even more severe than a lover, you love it, you submit to it, you hate it. You strangle it in secret, adorn it and paint it in brilliant colors like some insane idol, day by day you poison yourself with it. And afterwards, when the torture is complete, when you think you're finally free, there's already another roaring in the wings.

My dream would be to live on an island, nested in a rock, with huge, gentle lizards as my only readers, who would come, with their crenellated carapaces, to eat algae from my hand, with the wind and waves as the only music. There wouldn't be any more need to write there. We'd be naked, engorged with sunshine, at rest in a silence more beautiful than any book.

And love would be a tall black sorcerer with an ebony sex, shining with musky sweat, who would marry, upon my body, the rhythm of the sea. And I would go to sleep, linked by the rings of his long black pythons. White sorcerer, black sorcerer, what does it matter, as long as the magic transcends us.

To write is to kill, it's to roll naked in ash, it's to escape into suicide and madness. You spit in its face, second by second you tear from it its living secrets from rot and you die of it. I write to vomit myself as I was made, I write to perpetuate myself the way I was loved and wounded, caressed and resuscitated. No act is reasonable if it is not kindled, at the root of ourselves, by our hidden desires. They must be given a voice on pain of death.

— Grisélidis Réal, from "Why I Write,"
Gazette de Lausanne, 3 April 1971.

Your Name, Grisélidis

"In the alley, night just fallen, under a fine rain, so fine, your face touched by a sweet vapor perfumed with ripe apple. It comes from a huge, infernal cavern."

— Filipo de Pisis

They called her the little Egyptian demon. That was in the years before the war. Her father ran the Swiss elementary school in Alexandria, she must have been five or six years old. She remembers today how her mother would torment her, along with her two younger sisters, with over-strict ideas. Sometimes daily, or at least once a week, she'd make them line up on the bed, legs in the air, spread wide, and she'd inspect their little genitals. She'd say, "Ah! It's red! You'll be punished." The unfortunate girl wouldn't really know why she'd be punished like that, aside from having been the only one with this betraying redness. And there was a schoolmistress who had the students draw tables with little squares corresponding to the days of the month. When a student had been well-behaved, she had the right to draw a little yellow star. And when she had been mean, and admitted it, she would draw a little cross, or a little star, or a little flower, in black. And Grisélidis had a lot of little black stars in her school notebook. The schoolmistress said: "She is mean, she takes a whip or a lash, she beats her sisters and then she tells them stories of dragons and witches to scare them, she makes them suffer, she keeps them from sleeping at night." Grisélidis was forbidden to attend the big party at the end of the year. She was the demon of Egypt. That stayed in her head. Like a curse.

It's her mother who found this fantastic name for her, Grisélidis, in a fairly unknown Perrault fairytale. It was the story of a young peasant girl that a more or less misogynist prince had wanted to test, so he persecuted her even after marrying her. Vanquished by her resignation, her patience and her virtue, he finally set about making her happy. This tale of conjugal piety was in reality the version given by picture books in the nineteenth century. Perrault himself preferred to make fun of the malice of women: "It is not," said he, "that Patience is not a virtue among the ladies of Paris, but rather, that through a long tradition they have learned the science of compelling that virtue in their husbands." But Grisélidis never got that chance. All the fathers of her children forgot her. And she had had too many insane black men for lovers. She was often wounded, she took her revenge, and voilà. In any case, it is not by this beautiful name that she's best known here. On her door, she has embroidered, in red hearts, a suburban, matronly, first name: Solange. And underneath, she has simply indicated: Courtesan.

She lives in Geneva, in the Pâquis neighborhood, famous for its arsons, its lost girls, its full-moon nights, its bums and drunkenness. On this particular day she'd put on a little faux lizard bustier and black amber perfume. As always, the stereo was on: Russian gypsy songs, or Salim Halali, or a Gerry Mulligan jazz record. On the second floor of this particular ruin is a Judas with a Japanese lamp: the habitués know very well that if the lamp is lit it means the lady is busy, and that there is no use shaking this uncanny little bell until everybody in the building shows up; in any case, nobody in the building gives a shit. All there is to hear is stampedes, songs, and fistfights until morning. It's on Rue des Belles-Filles (Street of Pretty Girls), and, as we used to say, Evil Ways. Grisélidis had repainted her room in an unexpected way: color of almond and prawn.

She finishes by making up her eyes in black. Behind the painted dragons and the fans, you can see, through the kitchen windows, the roof of a protestant church, whose bells ring twice on Sunday mornings. Grisélidis has already glued scandalous posters on its door: she has always hated Calvin. I find her enchanted this morning: she has just sent an article in to a new hooker review, *Macadam*. She rattles her little Cambodian curtain made of straw pearls, laughs loud, gesticulates before the mirror of a ponderous Louis XVI armoire, goes looking for a trysting card game, with "streetwalker" printed in gold letters on it, she talks to me about her black little Moleskine, and disappears again and again into a backroom where at some point she put together a few bookshelves, crammed with a mess of books and papers. It is there that she writes her letters and piles up a boatload of articles devoted to prostitutes and their struggle.

Grisélidis has very black eyes. Attractive eyes, like eyes in a portrait. Photographs of her show her in a scarf with long black braids, Moroccan shawls, or bright silk dresses—like a Gypsy fiancée. You'd always have the impression she was dancing: her head almost upside down, her hair falling over her powerful shoulders, and her twisting hand doing a kind of flamenco. You'd imagine the faces of Czech violinists around her, with melancholic blue eyes, bony and leathern faces. With mustaches dyed black.

She has always loved, I think, glass jewelry. She used to have some charms that she called, a bit grandiloquently, her "pink diamonds of the desert"; or costume jewels, "Spanish cemeteries," which were shaped like flowers and made of yellow glass, with their two-bit shimmer, swinging around her neck. The littlest ones were the "drops of blood." She says that she wears jewelry every day, and that she changes it as often as she pleases: it's the Gypsy in her that wants that. Perhaps she's still dreaming of the slim Gypsy boys who would play guitar with a knife, who would wrap their bodies around her. Or she's thinking of old Tata in Munich, when he beat Sonja, insane with rage and humiliation, the whole war going to his head, having drunk too much of that lung-burning Steinhager.

She likes black best. She always has. When she lived in Germany, you'd see her in a slim black suit, in her pink diamonds of the desert. Or in a little sort of Chinese dress, with ivory satin lapels. But sometimes too, she'd be wearing nothing but a flowered peignoir, doing her eye makeup while drinking schnapps; those were the times in Schwabing, the artist neighborhood in Munich. When she went to jazz clubs, or the cafés where black soldiers went. With her faux rings or her long serpent bracelets with their green eyes. These days she puts a starfish in her hair to hide the holes: the Berber, a guy she loves and would die for, tore her hair out when he was demented with alcohol. She looked at him, right then, in the eyes, like a drowning cat.

Grisélidis has lived in nomad camps, surrounded by old, smashed buses, broken-down wooden caravans and ostrich flocks. She'd get into skyblue Cadillacs with her black lovers, at four in the morning, on Leopoldstrasse, dragging her two kids behind her. She called herself Mimi, at the "Erotic Bar." She sold Moroccan kif or Brazilian mescaline, which she took for seven months, before getting kicked out of Germany and brought in a van as far as Constance. Then, she was a whore in Schwabing, in the big red house, run by Big Mamma Shakespeare, a White Russian of at least fifty, monstrous and good, with her slip full of holes and her yellow hair.

Here is Grisélidis now, in her fifties herself. As indicated in the most recent federal population census, her precise business address is the Pâquis sidewalk. She has flouted the euphemism "domestic worker," and has indicated her profession as "courtesan," on the list of French-speaking writers, ever since she published *Black is a Color*, about her clandestine life in postwar Munich. She pays taxes, thoroughly disinfects her body at any sign of illness; it has not been that long since she caught syphilis; she was peppered, even on the palms of her hands and the soles of her feet, with tiny purple dots, as though marked by the thorns of a rosebush. Now she mixes penicillin with three glasses of red and one glass of bourbon. She's sovereign. Grisélidis has a laugh that is atrocious, vulgar, and profound. When she laughs, you always think she's shrieking. Like an animal. It's the laughter of a woman with her throat cut.

She loves messing with bourgeois women. Bitter wives and housework devotées. She can become terrible, filled with rancor and fury. She wrote to me one day, during the Paris-Geneva TEE (Trans Europ Express), "I feel triumphant. If the bourgeois ladies surrounding me only knew that I paid for the right to sit among them by expertly and patiently making immigrant laborers come, perfumed with sweat and wine! Saturday, day of rest among the populace, I got fucked by ten of them, including one of the worst, the Auroch, an enormous Spaniard, a prehistoric beast, terrifying and violent, with a child's appetite, gigantic balls like melons, and at the end, since he has a hard time getting there, despite his roars of enthusiasm, he jacks off in a lather of sweat, with infernal screams, Anda, Anda, Anda, and he pounds me against the wall enough to crack my head open. Thus, exhausted and victorious, do I quit the Hell of Ordinary Saturdays."

Now and again she'd send me perfumed letters, in her big, sumptuous handwriting. She spoke of those Turks with frightening dicks. Or of the herds of Arabs who would show up at her place, the drunks she kicked out, who'd come back to piss on her doormat for revenge. She spoke of Aloise, a woman from the sanitarium who painted huge blue eyes and huge mouths like vaginas, open and inert. She was enraged, superb; I always saw her as Caravaggio's Medusa, with her serpents unfurling, dark and vociferating, or as an attic Fury. She loved recounting her ferocities to me, the way women must have done to tolerant girls in the last century: they'd put madness in your nerves with martinets wielding whips of perfumed leather, silken cords for bondage and little bouquets of stinging nettle.

Grisélidis proclaims to anyone who'll listen that she lives her prostitution as a delinquency. She doesn't tremble from it, despite the intrigues of those who want so desperately for her to admit her sad condition. For her, misery has always been dispelled by the touch of a man. Maybe, with age, she isn't angry at anyone anymore. Not at her lovers from the black ghettos of Chicago or at the neighborhood girls or at the Berber, with his nervous breakdowns, when he'd punch her in the stomach because she dared to glance at other guys: the Berber drank as much as he did to give himself the courage to be evil. "So much for passion," she finally said, breathless, "you've got to save your own skin." She has forgotten the sarcasm, the cruelty, the betrayals. There is, decidedly, no cruelty on her lips, nor is there misery. She is so alone, at bottom, and yet so in love with all of her different lives, that you just start loving her. At one point something confused her among my questions. I was talking about voodoo dolls, with pins in them, to make men die. She said to me, brutally, "I could not even take revenge against a person who had killed my children."

She gave me her little black book. Her killing book. It is where she inscribes her johns, for all eternity. A few brief remarks, very useful, on the clients, prices, personal details. She pages through it like a nut when a guy calls from the phone booth downstairs. This little book is not the novel of her life as a whore. It's just a quick summation of tricking, and the erotic ways of men. She hides it near her bed. Like a diary. Or a dance card. Or an art of love for

Grisélidis Réal at a sex-worker's protest in the 1970s. Courtesy of Igor Schimek.

ill-begotten pleasures. Ovid had this charming remark for ladies in love: "Do not let light pass through all of the windows in your bedroom. Certain parts of your body do not benefit from being seen in daylight." Grisélidis, indeed, always closes the curtains that give onto the street, and she lights three candles. It's her little book of the penumbra.

It is neither more nor less than an instruction manual for johns, and it is what remains from the repetitive and awkward gestures, little cheats, the patience and tenderness. The little book is not obscene or cruel, though one might imagine at first sight that it could be. It exists simply because of lack of memory, it's her age that required it. It functions like a tattoo. Even if, in expressing so dryly these passions, in enumerating in such raw terms these manias, it means that there is nothing but bone in passion. Grisélidis, ever since her novel, writes no other book but this little black book. Methodical, she notes day by day the litanies of men who have come to fuck and come inside her and sometimes to love her, if one can love as quickly, as poorly, and as powerfully as one sometimes, all of a sudden, wants to. "These Moroccans," she wrote me one day, "beautiful, savage, and caressing, even in brutality, I'm going to end up falling in love with them." She always wrote about her lovers in vengeance and devotion at the same time.

Grisélidis has nothing left to hide: she says simply that she has recovered, found herself again. And her little book, certainly, could be placed among the city's tourist leaflets. Like a bible of delicacies. It could even be distributed in schools, where the teacher would set aside for it a few exemplary lessons, because it is very complete: you find in it the state of the ranks of Indian, Turkish, and Spanish laborers, of certain shameful practices and a few illnesses, household secrets, coquetries, interesting little shifts in the bedroom, from bed to bidet, from mirror to robe, bullshit and false currency, and even vain young black men. Here is a curious little guide for a trip to Switzerland, one Paulhan might have loved to write, had he dared.

Fundamentally, it's a book without an end. Like a bolero, it's a book that will exhaust the life of Grisélidis. She will die of it, of her adventures in cock, a bit incoherent and sad, she won't ever really know what will have become of all these men, whether they're still journeying, what chance might bring them together again or what memories they might still share. She writes them down as though she were never sure of having known them. Jean Genet, in *A Thief's Journal*, writes that he kept in his pocket a little record of his thugs, the ones he'd worked with, or the ones he'd known in prison and with whom he'd done projects or come to blows. "I am happy and calm," he wrote, "to know that they're alive, handsome and active, hidden in the shadows. In my pocket, the little book where their names are numbered is blessed with consoling power. It has the same authority as a penis. It's my treasure. To the complicity that unites us, I add a secret accord, a kind of standing pact, that few things, it would seem, could destroy, but that I know how to pro-tect, to handle with gentle fingers: it's the memory of our nights of love, or sometimes a brief lovers' conversation, or fondlings accepted with the smile and held-in sigh of a presentiment of passion." Perhaps, after all, Grisélidis gets something out of her secrets of those nights when the men are too drunk, or too tender. And perhaps her little book doesn't say anything about those things at all; maybe she has saved for herself these inexplicable moments that are the price of a whore, and her tomb.[1]

— Geneva, summer 1981

---

1. Grisélidis has also published *A Little Chronicle of Courtesans, Writing*, 12th edition. Bertil Galland: 1976.

1

THE INVISIBLE EQUATOR

Interviews with Grisélidis

> *She went out drinking and dancing as long as the money would last, and then she'd work the sidewalk, like me, when the money ran out. In German, they say:* Auf dem Strich gehen. *Exactly, "walking the line."*
>
> *A line, a cord, a line of happiness that crosses the world and upon which we all walk. A sort of invisible equator that traverses the earth and grazes our souls and feet.*
>
> — Grisélidis Réal, *Black is a Color*

1

Summer 1979

Grisélidis Réal: ...There's one who still comes back, unfortunately. Sometimes he stays for three hours. He can be hard for three hours but never ejaculate. And me, I've already tried everything, insults, tenderness, sweetness, encouragements, fits of rage. Everything, but there's nothing to be done, because he's addicted to his own punishment. You see what I mean. Anyway, this, I've explained it in detail right here. You'll see that it's in alphabetical order.

Jean-Luc Hennig: *What's his name?*

His name is Daniel... So, wait, let me see. Here: psychological cases. There's number one, here's number two, there's all this, you see? All this makes three pages of my little book.

And your little book, it wasn't for... It was for you, it was practical?

This is my Bible! I can't work without this!

Why can't you work without it?

I'll explain to you: when somebody calls, "Hello, can I come over?" I say yes, who is it? OK, it's Pierre, it's Paul, it's René, it's Roger, you know. Oh ok! I already hear the voice, if... And since they'll be here in three minutes, because the phonebooth is right down the street... Sometimes they show up immediately, I don't have time to close the book, to put it down, they're already ringing the bell. So you have to know where you are, because if not, he'll say, "So how much do I give you? Like last time?" And then sometimes, he'll lower the price by half. And then, you have an individual in front of you, you'll have to start from zero, everything, that means you do a kind of search of his body, where are his sensitive points, should you put your finger in his ass or not, should he should be sucked from the left, the right, in front, in back. I mean, all of the maneuvers, you have to search them out. And this, this takes time, and you risk making a few wrong moves, but in here, there are intimate indications... This little book, it's little, I don't have some huge book, I don't have the time to read a lot. It's reduced to the strict minimum, technical indications.

Are there a lot of con artists?

One time, I lost a Joseph, well I didn't totally lose him, but it lowered the price, because I didn't recognize him fast enough. He called me saying, "Can I come over?" I said sure, fine, I didn't ask his name, because I heard an Italian or Spanish voice. I said, it's a laborer coming for fifty bucks. So the Joseph arrived, and no luck: him, this one should have paid seventy, because he required a few little flourishes that I rediscovered through the course of our meeting. Well, he gave me a hundred and I gave him fifty back; it's obvious he was not going to give me back the change. I asked him his name. All of a sudden I got suspicious, I said to myself, son of a bitch, this is no ordinary laborer. Tell me what your nickname is again? He tells me Joseph. I said shit, it's the one who gave seventy francs. And now that I did it for fifty, he'll never give me seventy again.

You see, this little black book, you can see how useful it is. Yesterday, a man called me with a sort of Italian accent. I said, who's calling? It's Mario. I looked. Marios, there's only one. "Italian, mustache, suck, fuck. Eighty francs. Assfuck first." He says, I'll be there in a half hour. Oh! In a half hour I have the time to write a letter. A half hour passes, bell rings, and I see a young skinny guy, no mustache, looks really aggressive, overexcited, he jumps on me, I say son of a bitch! Either I wrote it down wrong or I forgot to write him down. He's Mario number two, I didn't write him down because he didn't come back often enough. Basically I didn't understand anything. Already on the phone he was putting on airs, saying, I could give a little more, that would be better. I said, What do you mean better. The price's completely correct. There's no need to increase or decrease. Then I see this young man arrive, I said, this can't be the same one. He started kissing me on the mouth, sticking his hand in my bra. He opens his fly. I go, Halt! The money! He says, what? If that's how it is, I'm leaving. I say, you'd better get out of here quicker than that, and I kicked him out, he was a just a horny freak who wanted to fuck. He thought he was an Adonis.

And Daniel?

Oh well. I wrote it here. This is a man who'll be hard for three hours. And here: he doesn't want to be brutalized. You have to be very gentle, very sweet, like a little girl, like you're two kids having fun in some field, like the forbidden childhood loves that he never had and that have stayed in him like a nostalgia. And then, at the same time, you have to reassure him, you still have to encourage him. So, I'm telling you, the sperm rises in his cock but it goes back down dry at the very moment it could have come out. This guy, he prevents himself from coming. And ever since he was little, he's been forbidden sexual pleasure, so he got stuck on this interdiction. In a way, it's easier for him to forbid himself to come than it is to just say look, mommy and daddy are mad at me, all of society's going to laugh at me or judge me or condemn me because I never took my pleasure. So he doesn't take it. But it's a horrible anguish. He really suffers atrociously. I pity him. He's a charming man, intellectual…

You also told me about a fat guy who demolished a mattress.

That's Fat Robert, he's noted down here. This is a man who has the courage to say: I go to hookers, I've gone all my life.

He's really fat?

Enormous! He's like this on one side, you know, we could go for a coffee in his bistro, he's like this! He's already murdered a bed, an armchair, and I'm worried about my bidet! *(Laughter.)*

Aside from the bed cracking, are there unexpected things?

Horrible things! One time, there was a sort of Spanish man who had a totally simple demeanor, nothing in particular about him. A laborer. But at the end he didn't come. So I brought him in front of the mirror, I did a little cinema for him. When you suck a man off in front of a mirror it flatters him, the woman on her knees in front of him, à la antique adoration. It's beautiful, he sees himself naked with a woman sucking his cock, a mirror game, it's splendid, and this always puts him back into shape. And since it's also tiring, it's awful to be on your knees, so after a while I say listen, let's go over to the bed. When you've kind of managed to get him in better condition in front of the mirror, you have to hope it won't fall down again right away, and on the bed, you continue and it's more comfortable. Sometimes it doesn't work, you have to put a finger in his ass... People will steal anything. They'll take this little thing for putting on shoes, people have taken my alarm clock, I don't know how many times, even little nativity figures. You've got to have your eyes everywhere. Somebody stole a red garter belt, now I only have the bra in that color. An old Spanish guy, dead drunk. I don't know what he did with it. Anyway, he had the balls to show up here again after doing that. I said, I won't have you again. I couldn't even tell him that in Spanish, and he didn't understand French. If that was the case, he must have been so trashed he couldn't even remember. Yeah, so this man had difficulties, totally Spanish and on top of that a laborer. So I put a finger in his ass with Vaseline, and then I feel his prostate hardening, but a little bizarrely. There were, like, rings. So I said, huh, this is kind of special, anatomically. He has the right to be a little special. He had told me, "I can do anything." These laborers, they speak bad French! I concluded that he wanted to ejaculate in my mouth. I signaled him yes. I worked on him, I worked on him, thank God, a hard-on. Afterwards, I felt something rising, I said, ok, it's the finale, the horse can smell the stable. And then, son of a bitch, I run to the bathroom as usual and I spit what? Piss. It took me the whole day to pull myself together after that. I brushed my teeth six times, I sucked candies, I drank whiskey. I couldn't forget it. Mentally, I still had this idea that someone pissed in my face without asking my permission. This is something that's just not done. What a bastard, come on!

Les Pâquis is really a jungle, huh?

Well yeah! And when there's a full moon, we can't even talk about it!

A full moon?

Because they've drunk so much, and then it's knife fights, screaming, stabbings, and cops descending on the place nonstop, it's horrible! One night, I go to sleep at three in the morning, I was going to sleep, I hear somebody screaming Help, help! I said great, another doll getting stabbed by her pimp, I put the cover over my ears to go to sleep and all of a sudden, I hear Fire! I say to myself there's fire somewhere. I didn't move. All of a sudden, I hear something completely insane, I go to the window in my nightgown, I put on my glasses and I see firemen setting up an enormous ladder at 4 in the morning. There were plumes of black smoke, it was right here, next door to Fat Robert. And I saw girls, naked or in nightgowns, in nylon babydolls, being carried down on the ladders. Apparently they had the right to yell fire, they'd been burning. And to the right, at the same time, there were two drunks in the process of killing each other, one choking the other, demanding his wallet. But you know this neighborhood! I'm going to live someplace else, I can't stand it anymore!

How many times has someone pissed on my doormat, torn off my nameplate, burned my door, it's too much! And people call you at 6 in the morning, at 8, at midnight, at 3 a.m., no matter what time, with thick, mocking voices to ask if you're asleep.

Have you ever worked with boys?

No, I've never done that. Look, I manage by myself. I don't even have porno magazines or pictures. One time a guy came, he was looking through everything. Don't you have any dirty mags? You don't have dirty pictures, you don't have this, you don't have that? I said hang on: Strip! Put your clothes here—because I don't like them getting mixed up with mine—I told him ok, we're gonna go bathe, I scrubbed him down, I brought him back here, I said, the photo, it's right here, and I brought him in front of the mirror, I sucked him as usual, he was totally delighted. I said, you see, it's like the movies, no need to look at a photo. He was totally happy. He thanked me, said it was incredible. He never asked for a photo again.

You always wash them first?

Before and after. You discover a lot of things. Some of them have warts, some of them have pustules, more or less oozy, you have to see everything, everything, everything. Some of them have hernias, some have growths that look like cancer. You have to know what you're dealing with.

Have there sometimes been handicapped people?

Yes, there are some who come, brought by a friend, with two crutches, a leg in plaster. It happens.

Are there guys who have to be carried?

Yes, carried up the stairs. But what's horrible about handicapped or infirm people, it's that they're always very aggressive. They feel diminished, they suffer, they feel that they're not like other people. This makes them angry, enraged, from the get-go. And they only get hard with a lot of trouble. It makes them aggressive to have to face that it's not going to work most of the time. You have to calm them down, cajole them, reassure them. You see, it's all an art. A good whore has to work as quickly as possible. But every gesture, every word, every smile must seem to last the maximum.

The maximum?

Yes, amount of time. A caress, a gesture, a smile, it has to feel like that smile will last an hour. In reality it'll last three seconds. You see, you must never rush people. You can't leave them hanging either, because after that it won't work anymore. It's an art. They have to have the impression that you've almost loved them, that you've taken care of them, that you've adored them, that you've caressed them, that you've released them, made them explode, that they're totally blooming. It's an impression. And in fact, they've experienced that in a particular moment, but in reality, it's all illusion, because finally, you don't love them more than this. My God, you're so glad when they're gone! It's terrible.

How old are your oldest clients?

There are some over eighty.

You're kidding!

No! You always think they're going to pass out in your arms. There are a few, they start to have trouble breathing. You say to yourself, I better not end up with a cadaver on top of me. We'd better at least try to arrange a way out, especially if it's a guy who weighs a certain amount, you don't want to find yourself stuck under a dead man. You always calculate a little with this. Some of them, you have the impression it's the last time they can fuck before the tomb, and incidentally, they don't hide from it.

What do they say?

"Oh, *ma chérie*, darling, you're giving me life, thanks to you I feel alive. The doctor forbade me to make love, but you see, it's marvelous, you've given me life, you've given me youth, you've given me love." Which means, I didn't croak, but phew that was a close one.

They come day and night?

Oh yes! At six in the morning, or at 3 a.m., they want pleasure. So the bell rings!… The bell, do you want me to ring it? When it rings at 6 in the morning, I run out in a nightgown, haggard, I don't see clearly, I see some kind of zombie weaving like this, dead drunk, I say come on, who do you think you are? *(Murmuring:)* "Oh! Solange, I want you! I say, get the fuck out of here, let me sleep. What a nightmare! Quelle horreur! An hour later, the phone rings, or it's the same guy come knocking again, he thinks it's 3 in the afternoon, and it's 8 in the morning, because they've been crawling through every bar in the neighborhood.

You never take them in the morning?

Absolutely not!

What time do you start?

At 3 in the afternoon. That's already plenty early. Some come at 10 to 3 or even at 2.

Until what time?

Until I can't take it anymore. When I need money to pay bills and there are clients, I have to take them, otherwise it would be stupid. Sometimes, you have them until 2 or 3 in the morning. There are women who are slaves to the job. Not me. The less I do, the better. That's my slogan. There's no point to work like an animal, afterwards you're totally used up, you need six months in the hospital, or you get cancer and die at fifty-five. That's not cute. You start to feel like a dump, a fuck machine. The cash is always spent pretty fast. Me, half of what I earn goes to peaceful revolution, to fuck the whole world, pamphlets, magazines, meetings, poetry. It takes its toll. At least it gives me pleasure. The rest is for me. You see. I make money, but this money, I do what I want with it. If I want to buy anarchist papers, which I have up to the ceiling, and distribute them to people for free—there are plenty of clients who leave with enormous packages of documentation under their arm, because they want to or because I force it on them, you're gonna read this, you'd better take this. I say, take this, put it in your office, put it in your house, in front of your parents, in front of your friends, and voilà. It's the truth about banks, war, torture, prison.

You give them an article?

I make them take it. I say, now you're gonna read this. I say it in front of them.

Do they think you're a little strange?

Oh, certainly! That's why they come back. It piques their curiosity to the quick. They don't understand anything. There've been guys who told me, "Oh! You've got reading material!" Like it's a crime to read. Oh la la! This? I say, it's nothing. There are another fifty boxes of it in the Gare de l'Est in Paris. Because I emptied out my studio over there. So they see this, and they say, Oh la la, you have weird stuff to read! They start bitching and moaning. And I see that they hesitate to open their fly. They say to themselves, this lady's an anarchist, she has reading material that calls us into question, because we're bankers, well-positioned gentlemen, and it fucks with them. But I'm overjoyed.

I say, hang on honey, I'm still going to fuck you in the ass, I'm going to suck your cock, I'm gonna slap you two or three times and on top of all this you get to look at Ziegler's book, it's a great deal.

There haven't been any who got angry and left?

Yes, some got enraged, crazy. Back in the day, I had a piece of writing against nukes. So the fellow gets all red like a lobster, he started roaring in my kitchen, in the hallway, in the bedroom, saying nuclear power, we're gonna get it no matter what, and the truth is it's the only solution. I let him scream, I looked at him, he was getting more and more enraged. In the end I said, not at all, there are other solutions, there are gentler sources of energy, they haven't tried everything yet, it will come, and anyway it will be the good things that win out. He was in a fit of anger. He fucked fine, but I never saw him again. Some don't come back because of what I read and the articles on the wall. So much the better. Let them think at home, jack off in the shitter.

And clients who can't come, who leave disappointed?

Oh! There's a little shit with a huge mustache, a Spanish guy. Him, he never comes. And since I have no memory, I took him back four or five times without remembering that it was the same guy. So him, he comes in, takes his clothes off, and he starts fucking. And it can go on like this for ten minutes, fifteen, twenty minutes, a half hour, forty-five minutes, an hour, hour and a half. He goes on and on and he never comes, never. He's hard, obviously, but he never ever comes. He proposes to pay more, so I insult him, I pick a fight, it's horrific, I'm thinking he likes this, you see. And he doesn't want to get the fuck out of here, he doesn't want to put his clothes back on, I mean this is really misery, you know?

So what do you do?

I become like a fury, I scream so much, I become so terrifying that in the end he is forced to put his clothes back on and leave. He's forced to because... Oh I would kill him on the spot! And now I won't have him back. There are four or five I don't have back, but you don't realize how much there is like this! It's a jungle!

You told me once, "Without music, it's hard...."

It's hard. When you have some excellent jazz on, it's so gorgeous to give a blowjob in rhythm, it really works for embellishments. If there's a good solo on, after you've done the Japanese fire ants, you can squeeze his balls in time with the music. It helps! After you lick, you suck, the guy ejaculates in music.

What are Japanese fire ants?

Oh! It's a thing of mine I invented. *(Laughter.)* You have the guy's penis in your mouth, on one side you press a little at the base of the balls, you hold the scrotum in your right hand and you squeeze delicately, you apply little pressures because it stimulates the whole organism, you soak the penis in saliva, it has to be really slippery. With your left hand, you do the Japanese fire ants, that means you go like this...

You scratch?

Absolutely not! You slide. It's like little ants walking on the cock near the head, you go down and up very delicately, turning a little so that it's covered in saliva and at the same time you suck, and you exert delicate little pressures with your right hand underneath. It's an art.

This is why nobody better come to us to tell us we're not useful, I've had clients many times who told me, Nobody in the world has ever done that to me so well. You see we're great artists, it's like playing the piano or the harp or the guitar, you have to have technique.

And this red dog leash here?

Once when I was depressed I wanted to buy myself a little dog, but since he cost a thousand francs, I renounced that, I'd rather buy myself books or records. So this dog leash, it's for beating people. It's very useful. It was pretty expensive, actually. Real leather.

Do you use it often?

Oh, sometimes. Before I used a belt, but it wasn't as good for whipping.

Where do you whip them?

Everywhere. On the thighs, around the penis, on the ass, the back, even in the face. Everything works. They love it. I'm serious! You whip them standing up in front of the mirror. This way they can see themselves getting whipped. They see this red leash covering them in lashes. They see themselves getting hard. It makes my work easier. *(Laughter.)* One time, there was a guy lying down here on the ground, you see that straw stool! He was a maso. I was so sick of him that I took the stool, I removed what was on top of it, I shoved it in his face, I put my foot on it, I crushed his face under the stool while I was whipping and insulting him, and that stool worked great by itself.

Do you strangle them?

Oh yes! The young man I just had, I didn't know what to do to him. Finally, I took his belt and strangled him with it. And then I said, you know, I could kill you if I wanted to. So his eyes were drowning in rapture and fear, and I said to myself, after all, if I squeezed a little harder and a little longer.... But then, what are you going to do with a corpse? And anyway, he's just a poor young man and I don't want to kill him.

Why did you say to me, "This little black book is my revenge"?

It's my revenge because, when you've suffered like it's not possible, when you have to be glued to their balls for an hour until something comes out, well, afterwards I give them the phone number. There are some, I know they'll come back, and there are some I don't know, and at that moment I write them down. They're written down for eternity.

The second time?

Some are written down right away. When I can see that they might come back, and it's such a pain, they need so many specialties, I write them down right away because after, I forget. It's my revenge. When I'm miserable, at zero, I reread my little black book and I laugh by myself. I say look, they're recorded in here and they don't know it. I laugh! I have a great time!

How long have you been doing it?

It's been two years.

Have you noticed things going better now?

No, but I turned fifty this summer. I'm losing my memory, in my life I've had so many overdoses, failed suicides, I've been gutted so many times, everything you can think of, lung operations, everywhere. I don't have any memory left, I forget everything, everything, everything. It's too much work to try to remember things, this is a memory aid, that's all.

Nobody's ever looked at you through the window?

Oh yes, yes. One afternoon, I had had one of my regulars, a gentleman of a certain age, very kind. I'd brought him to the sink, I'd washed him and everything. Then, once he's blown his load, I bring him back to the kitchen, I wash him again, I dry him. He was naked, reading articles, and I was on the bidet, all at once I lift my head, like this, by chance, and I see two guys on the roof of the church, they were repairing it, roofers. Young guys in blue outfits. Overalls. I gagged. They'd been watching a long time already. But they must see all kinds of things with their job. I was kind of embarrassed, but what was I supposed to do, my hands full of soap, my ass soaking wet, naked on the bidet, straddling it. So I saw them laughing, they went Woo-hoo at me, and I made big motions, hey, hi! The client, his back was turned, he didn't see anything. He would have gone nuts if he'd known there were two young guys who'd watched everything lying on their stomachs on the roof of the church.

It's the only time that's ever happened to you, you've never found yourself in front of people...

Never! That's why I didn't even think of looking at the church that time, you know? And anyway, I never want to look at the church anyway, I must have wanted to look at the sun or see if the weather vane turned… or my flowers in the window. All of a sudden I see two guys on their stomachs on the roof eyeballing me…

They were standing their ground?

Well, as soon as they'd seen that there was a little show going on, obviously they didn't want to miss a thing! But it was really funny. We made big signals to each other. Big smiles…

Tell me the story of Old Joseph.

Old Joseph is a Swiss German who lives in Geneva. He gets older and older. He's close to his eighties. He's well preserved because he does a lot of cycling…

Does he come here often?

Oh, he comes pretty often, yes. He pays 80 francs. He's in my black book. But now, I've added The Vampire to his entry, because I just did that to him the last time he came over…

Oh! Tell me about The Vampire… It's a new thing you do?

Never done it before! It was an inauguration. It was the first time in my professional life as a whore and artist, because there has to be art everywhere. So it's really an invention. A creation. It's like somebody who works in fashion having created a new pattern, I created something completely new, The Vampire…. I didn't know that what was called for would be The Vampire, because I'd never even thought of it, I didn't even know it existed. When he came over, I took him in as usual. We go wash up, and then we get in front of the mirror, I suck, I stroke his balls and everything. He's barely hard, and you can't demand too much of him at his age, he's tired of standing up and I'm tired of being on my knees too, frankly, so we get on the bed. And he stretches out. I continue sucking, and here in general I do the Japanese fire ants with a finger in his ass, but unfortunately he wasn't hard at all, at all. So I said to myself, do Japanese fire ants on what? Wind? There's no point! He won't even feel them, he's not hard... So my imagination leapt, I said, I have to find something else, I'm going to try doing The Vampire. It came to me like that, lightning... magnesium in my head, I said, let's see how this works! So I blocked off my breathing, I blocked off my hands, I blocked off Joseph's cock in my mouth and I became like a siphon. I sucked with all my might. And he wasn't hard! Nothing! After a few seconds or one or two minutes, I don't know how long you can hold it without exhaling, without letting out the breath you've been holding, and all of a sudden, I felt something coming. So now I couldn't let go, absolutely not. But this something had such a special taste that in my memory, my practical memory, I can't retrieve this sensation, I said, this, it's not piss, it's not sperm, but what is it? My god, *quelle horreur*, it's blood! Too bad, I had to not let go, because otherwise the whole thing was fucked. So I continued doing The Vampire, I inhaled, inhaled, inhaled, inhaled with desperate energy, saying to myself the whole time, I'm gonna die, it's asphyxia, no more oxygen in my lungs. I'm gonna die in the act, but oh well, I can't let go... Well, after the blood came sperm, a few miserable drops of sperm, he's eighty years old, they finally came out after a lot of work, but.... Oh! I ran out to spit at high speed. Obviously, I spat, it was bright red. And old Joseph, all perky, tells me, you see, you really had your work cut out for you, because at least he's honest, he doesn't try to sneak around things, he said to me, I gave you a lot of work this time. I said no, of course not Joseph, don't worry! You see, it works very well.

He said that amazing thing to you…

He said, you see, I can still do it at my age. He says that to me every time. He says, it's because I was athletic all my life. So me, because I'm a little sly after all, a little vain let's say, I said, but what about your wife? Do you still make a little love with her? Meaning, if you did, then you'd come around bothering me a little less, because sometimes I really can't take it anymore. So he says yes, yes, yes. Sometimes. When she's not too tired. Because she's old, his wife. Maybe she's the same age as him. This is why I say that the wives of our clients should bring us flowers and thank us on their knees for the job we've done in their place. I can't see old Joseph's wife on her knees in front of the mirror…

Does he look glad afterwards?

He's illuminated, he's thirty years younger. He's happy, he's so happy! He's so reassured about his virility, the tiny bit of youth he has left… It's fabulous to see Joseph's face when he's finished, when he's putting his clothes back on, when he's leaving. And then the way he kisses me on the cheeks, the way he holds my hand, the way he thanks me. He says, see you next time!… It's marvelous. I get much more than money out of it, because I don't get that much money. This is why he comes to me, because no woman in the neighborhood except the sixty-three-year-old ladies twice my size, and even older than that—aside from that he wouldn't be able to find anyone to do a job like that! And anyway, I'm the only one who's done The Vampire on him, I'm sure of that. He walked out of here, you should have seen it… Like a young man! He gamboled down the stairs.

When they open the door, you're not the type to say, "On your knees!"?

Oh no, not at all! Not at all! *(Laughter.)* Cruelty is exhausting! It taxes your nerves… *Au contraire*, I open my arms, I take them in, I kiss them on the cheek. Sometimes they rush full speed to kiss me on the mouth, because they see me getting undressed right away, but it annoys me.

You don't like kissing them on the mouth?

I don't love them, I don't love these men! I don't feel love for them!

You never kiss?

Sure, the minimum. The strict minimum. But it's no fun. These people, they'll stay glued to your face for three hours. And during all that time they're not even hard!… It's a concession I make to move the work along. Or to please a poor guy who is so frustrated it actually hurts me to see. Since I see poor Turks, poor Arabs who come here twice a month, seventy kilometers on a motorbike, in the rain. And then I ask them, kindly, I say, don't you have a wife? You don't have anyone? You can't find a nice fiancée? They say No, nobody, French people: racists! So come on, look, I'm not gonna refuse them a little kiss. That would really be inhuman. Plus, they give me a hundred French francs. For them, that's a lot. Plus the kilometers on the motorbike and everything, you can't be too vile after all… But all the saliva, everything, all these badly-shaven faces chafing you all over, all that, it's pointless. Pointless. You have to focus on the essential. The man, what he wants is to get hard and ejaculate. Voilà. For everything else, you talk, you light candles, you put music on, you caress them right and left, tac tac, and there you have it. Yesterday I had this man, he didn't even penetrate me because he didn't have time. I said I would suck him, he said No, no… At first I thought it disgusted him, I said, that's odd, you don't like it? He said neither yes nor no.

I said huh, there's something going on here. I stroked his thighs, his chest, his shoulders, his knees, his balls a little bit, not too much. Afterward I had the unfortunate idea to press up against him, he felt one of my breasts against his cock, I got back up, I said, you want to come in where it's warm, that means in the pussy. He put a hand on his cock, he said ah! Ah! Well voilà. It was already too late.

What was this one's name?

He never told me his name, he was a Spanish laborer. So he left. He wasn't mad at all. He said, see you next time. We kissed each other on the cheek.

And the last time you really kissed somebody? Somebody you loved?

Well, it was with my Berber, two and a half years ago. I remember a fabulous kiss he gave me in a taxi when he was deported from France, and we were going to Gare du Nord to leave for Belgium. Well he kissed me, it was a devastating farewell kiss. But this was love! I would have kissed him for ten years, day and night, without eating, without pissing, without sleeping, nothing. This kiss gave me that much pleasure, it was so real, it was so gorgeous. It was better than making love, almost.

And you're dead to kisses ever since?

I'm like everyone! Come on! If my Berber kisses me, it's always going to be my Berber kissing me.

2

Spring 1981

Jean-Luc Hennig: *So the black book has expanded?*

Grisélidis Réal: It's expanded, certainly. There are wonderful things in there. There's the famous Maurice.

What's the famous Maurice?

Here! "Maurice, psychiatrist, intelligent, handsome and kind. Masochist. Very hard erection; comes under torture. Deep assfuck; bite, scratch, pinch nipples, handjob, suck. 200 F and up. Trample on him a little. Very dark, not too tall. Black eyes and hair." Pretty extraordinary, don't you think?

So psychiatrists come to see you?

He's an attendant at the asylum. He's the one who told me that he works with psychiatrists. You think they don't go crazy from treating people who are deranged?

Is he nice?

Adorable! When I was getting death threats over the phone, he told me, if this ever happens again, you can call me no matter what time it is, and I'll come right away to defend you. And then, when I had syphilis, you know, first degree... Well, these stupid bitches, I warned them to be careful, I told them, it's my duty to tell you that I'm sick, because the guy who gave this to me, he's still running around. So I'm in treatment, right. You see, honesty. Them, they went and told all the clients, don't go to this woman, you see, she has a horrible disease. This was when I already had the certificate to prove I wasn't contagious, because I had gotten one to confirm it, and I went a month without touching a single client. I was living on my savings. So, this unfortunate man, he comes over. Since his wife has died of brain cancer, he's very unhappy. All of a sudden, he calls me in the middle of the night, can I come see you, I'm depressed. I say sure, come right away. It was 1, 1:30 a.m, when he left my place, the bars weren't closed. All of a sudden he calls me up in a shattered voice. "Listen I have to tell you something." I said, well what? "Look, I just left your place, I wanted to have a drink somewhere in one of the bars, and these women jumped on me saying, come to our place, come with me, Maurice." Because they know him well. He said no, no, it's already done, I've just been with Grisélidis. So one of these women says to him, What? *Quelle horreur*! She's sick! She has syphilis, you shouldn't have gone! So he called me, he was on the fifth floor below me. I was annoyed, I said, Maurice you know perfectly well, you know me, I'm honest, if I really still had some disease, well, I wouldn't have given it to you. You can come over and I'll show you my certificate of noncontagion, I can show you the prescriptions, all the penicillin I took, nine million or nine hundred units in a month and three weeks later I was a wreck. I couldn't take it anymore. And the syphilis was killed. You see, this poor guy, they'd plunged him into anguish like that, out of pure meanness, so that he wouldn't come see me anymore, so that I'd lose all my clients, so that I'd lose my living.

Did he come back?

Yes, he came back not too long ago. He's the one who said, hurt me. Hurt me a lot, but with love. Sweet!

And you hurt him?

My God, it's tiring to hurt someone. You have to get his imagination moving.

But with him, how do you do it?

Well, ok, I scratch him, I pinch him, I slap him, what do you expect me to do? I twist his toes, I bite him, I try to hurt him, it's difficult, and also, you have to… pinch the tips of his nipples. He likes that a lot, but it really hurts.

You don't use equipment?

No. It's not necessary. And then I finger him really deeply. And when I hurt his poor nipples so badly he goes Oh! You're insane, you're insane, it's unbearable! So I say Shut up. It's doing you good, isn't it! Yes, yes it is. So he screams, he trembles, it's awful. And the more he trembles the more I have to hurt him, to keep things moving forward.

And the Belgian in gabardine, what's that story?

You see, since we went to the Palais des Nations on October first, and there was a debate at the university, everyday, everyday the phone was ringing here nonstop. One day, there was a man who called at 2 in the morning, he says, ok, I'm Belgian. Can I come over? I say to him of course, but I don't receive in the morning. Come at 3 in the afternoon. So I'll come tomorrow. I say fine. There were people coming through here nonstop, journalists, sociologists, clients, it was endless. So the next day I wasn't quite ready, at ten to three the doorbell rings, and I see a man in beige gabardine at the door. He looked a little sad. I said, are you the Belgian gentleman? He said yes, yes. I said, you shouldn't come at ten to three, you should come at three. I was naked under a towel, you understand, I was just getting out of the shower. Honestly!

He preferred you like that!

I said no. Ten minutes later, I was ready, my eyes were done, by some miracle. This man comes back. Come in! I almost had to push him. I said, a timid one! He didn't move. I said, come on in, make yourself at home. Oh! I hadn't gotten dressed, to speed things along. I had a robe on and was naked underneath. When you do a client, there's no point getting dressed to get undressed five minutes later. I said to myself, he's going to be here any second, I only have time to do my eyes.

So this man was here, I said come in, make yourself at home. I closed the curtains, I lit the Chinese lantern, see, it's romantic. I brought out the sheets from under the cushion, I spread them out, I put the blue cushion out, the one I always use for the clients, because the others are mine, and I was even going to open my robe to move things along... That way, they're at least a little hard before getting their clothes off, it activates things. And the man still wasn't moving, he had his gabardine on. I said, honestly, this one's a dumbass. He's paralyzed! I said, well come on, take off your clothes! So he said, but I'm a journalist. I said, but that makes no difference, all kinds of people come to see me, lawyers, doctors, jurists—he didn't move. All of a sudden I felt a glimmer. Well come on, are you here as a journalist or as a client? Oh no! As a journalist! Oh God! I said, I beg your pardon, what a nightmare! *Quelle horreur*! I hurried up and closed my robe, I tied it twice around, I folded the sheets back up, the cushions, opened the curtains…. I was completely panicked, I said, listen, come into the kitchen, can I get you a drink? We each drank a whisky. He was white as a sheet. Afterward, he said, you wouldn't happen to have any documents on homosexual prostitution? I said of course, I have everything. So we went into the other room, I gave him everything I had, I never saw those books or documents again, or the gentleman either. I think those were the most terrifying fifteen minutes of his life. You see, he was a homosexual journalist, and he was thinking that any minute I would jump on him to rape him, you can see the anguish of this poor man!

Are you sometimes scared?

Oh! Everything's calculated in such a way so that I don't get myself killed. When you have a man here and you tell him to take his clothes off, he could have a gun in his pocket, a jacknife, a razor, who knows, so I light my candles, which means, I turn my back, you see, it's like in a cavalcade: the trainer, he puts on an act, he keeps his eyes open… These people, they have eyes in the back of their heads. So I watch the guy when it looks like I'm just lighting my candles. This way, I can see how he behaves. If he's taking his clothes off calmly, it's good. But he has a weird air about him, if he has his hand in his pocket and he's waiting to jump on me and kill me, well, in this kind of moment I manage…

But it's already happened, like in that Italian film about Véronique, you see the cop come in, put his weapon down on the night table and say, "I never pay. If you don't want trouble, don't kick up any shit!"

No, not exactly, I mean cops, I've got one who comes as a client, but he pays. Yeah sure, it takes him a very long time to get hard, I even have to blow out the candles, you see what I mean! It has to be total darkness, or only one candle out of three, but he pays.

How old is he?

He's between forty and fifty. But one time, at 5 in the morning, there was a man who'd gotten stopped in his car, when I had my studio in the old city. He said to me, ok, how much? It was 5 in the morning, I said, I'm going home, I've had enough, that's it. He said, but I'm from the police, so you're coming to my place, I'll give you 50 francs and if you don't come I'll make trouble for you. But I didn't go. I said, I don't give a shit if you're the police or not, I'm done working tonight, I'm going home to sleep. I didn't want to hear anymore.

You've never been raped?

Oh la la! The rapist! So I was walking one night. It was already 2 in the morning. And I hadn't made any money. Because some nights it doesn't work. And there's competition. There are young girls, eighteen years old, and I'm gonna be fifty-two. There are even sixty-three-year-old women. So you know, sometimes tricking's hard. At night, the women, they're all next to each other. Like a flowerbed. And the men, they go toward the freshest ones. I was walking, and I passed by "The Venetian," I turned a little to the left, well no, I hadn't yet rounded the corner, and a young blond guy came out of a café, because it was the time that all the cafés close, a young blond kid with curly hair, good-looking, he falls into step with me and says, Do you have a student rate? I said it depends! You have to always say either yes or no, to see what comes out, to see if the guy has cash, if he doesn't have any, if he's an immigrant, if he's Swiss or

a foreign tourist, does he have cash or not, you have to see everything. You have to see if he's drunk too much, if he wants to cheat
you, you have to see if he's a murderer or a cop or an escaped convict
or a drunk, I mean, you have to see everything in five seconds. In
five seconds, what am I saying? A millisecond! And anyway, men
who walk next to you, you've already been able to see a fair amount
of things, and you can hear what's going on in him by the sound of
his voice. I walked a little more on purpose. He says, yeah, I'm kind
of broke, I'm a little depressed, I'm not rich. I say, you know, all the
same I can't go below a certain price. Because that's just not done.
We stayed with fifty francs. That's already misery. That's the immigrant laborer price, you know?

Turks?

No, Turks are a hundred French francs because they work in
France. But an immigrant laborer working in Switzerland can give
fifty Swiss francs to a woman my age. There are even some miserable
girls who go for that low a price, and they're twenty-year-olds, but
it's to buy drugs. So I took this young man home with me. We
came into the vestibule, I turn the light on right away; I don't want
to stay in darkness. We had barely gotten inside, he hadn't yet, he
was behind me. And I hear this: "Ok, I'm gonna rape you. I need
to make love and I'm in a rush, so hurry up. I don't have time to
waste." I said fuck, just my luck. So I didn't lose my composure, I
said Ok, as normal, have a seat, do you want to have a little drink
or something? Miraculously, I had a beer in the fridge. I never have
any around because of my cystitis. Beer's a killer for cystitis. I had
cystitis for twenty years, so you see… Well, he was already pretty
shocked that I said yes, that dampened his mood, he would have
preferred me to yell for help so he could really rape me with con-
viction. So I had already won the first round. I go into the kitchen,

I open the beer as slowly as possible, I arrive back here with two glasses, I sit down next to him, very maternal, very conciliatory, I say to him, hey, good health, we toast. I'd lit some candles. I was in an anguish, I was trembling, but I didn't show it. So in the end, he told me his life story, his mom was a prostitute also, he and his brother were neglected, they weren't loved, more or less abandoned, his wife was in the hospital, she was waiting to have a kid, I mean a whole story. I let him talk and I added things. I said, oh, my poor little muffin, what sorrow! Oh! Really, was it like that? You shouldn't worry too much, it'll work out. I said to myself, I'm buying time, I'm buying time. So he says to me, couldn't we get a little more comfortable. All at once I lean toward my clock, I say good lord it can't be! It's already 3 in the morning, oh! 3 in the morning!

You understand, me at my age, I'm tired, I can't take it anymore. Oh la la, 3 in the morning. You know, I would gladly make love with you, really, I promise you, it would be amazing, but I just can't, you see it would really be a shame to do it in this condition, I wouldn't do a good job, it would be a shame. You see! So him, he must have felt that I was exaggerating a little, but since he had already been here an hour, and he'd told me his life story, his aggression had at least kind of... deflated. He couldn't pack the same punch he would have at the start.

He was young?

Very young. It's the worst, the young ones, I won't even take them anymore.

How old was he?

Oh! He was maybe 23. So I took him by the shoulders, I said, listen honey, forgive me, okay, come back when you want to, you can feel at home here, but you have to let me sleep. I used an anguished voice. He didn't insist. I led him tenderly toward the door, I kissed him on both cheeks, twice on each cheek, I said ok, goodnight, forgive me. I asked his forgiveness so much and nothing was even my fault, and he left. I said ouf! And I never saw him again. Never.

Do you still see handicapped people?

Of course. I have some who keep coming. So look, there's one who called me, I can't sit down, I can't walk, I can't lie down. I said my god, but what's left for him! So I'm home, you have to come to my place. Oh la la! I said to him, listen, I would gladly come to your place, but right at this moment I don't have a lot of time. I can recommend a friend of mine who is a stunning woman, extraordinary, she's even better than I am, Odette. You can see her very soon. So I say to him, I'll give you her phone number, and if for some reason it doesn't work out, you can call me back. He never called me back. I saw Odette recently and I said, did a handicapped gentleman call you by any chance, sent by me, named Henri, she said yes, yes. I went, and it worked out for me, because my man had made things miserable for me, he got me so mad, it was Sunday, I said there's nothing to be done, I have to get the fuck out of here so I won't see this guy anymore, and I spent the whole Sunday with him. Not a lot happened from the sexual point of view, but he enjoyed the company of a nice woman for a whole Sunday, he made her cakes, they drank tea, they drank champagne, I mean, for him it was a magical Sunday. Because Odette talked to him, carressed his head, certainly kissed him on the cheeks. She even tried to get him hard, maybe he couldn't do it, but at least he had the illusion of a Sunday in love.

How old was he?

Oh! He's not that young. He must be over fifty.

Your alarm clock got stolen again?

Oh that's a whole story. Look, one time I bought a red one, thinking, I'm myopic, I'll be able to see the red from far away. All it took was a moment not paying attention and bam. No more alarm clock. Doesn't matter if it's red, blue, or green anymore. So I bought myself another, a nice little one and I watched it like a hawk. Nobody stole that one off me. So one day a tiny little Portuguese guy comes in here, minuscule. I don't know why these poor guys are always like dwarves. They're so tiny you can barely see them. But this one was an artist, this little Portuguese man. Because he came in here, he gave me fifty francs, and then all grandiose, he gave me an additional five Swiss francs. I said, but why? Oh yes yes, it's a present, you can go have a drink somewhere, I mean, I said my God, how kind of you! That's how he put my disdain to sleep, which I realized only afterward. So I said to myself, what a sweet guy, and I stopped looking at the alarm clock and everything else, he put me in a state of confidence. In the time it took me to wash half my ass, all of a sudden he was dressed, he wanted to get going immediately, he was in a big hurry to get home to sleep, so I said goodbye to him and everything, and I come back here, no more alarm clock. I said this one really got me, with his five Swiss francs! What can I say, I've had I don't know how many socks stolen, the last guy who was looking at this with languorous eyes, I gave it to him, I said here, take it, I have plenty in the drawer. It costs eighty centimes at Migros, but these pathetic fools, they have to steal this off me so they can think they've got something of mine. I think that certain men are bothered by paying to make love. But if they didn't pay they'd never make anything. So they take a little thing, as consolation. Don't you think?

Have you ever been given counterfeit money?

Oh, Czech money. I didn't take it, that money has absolutely no value.

Are there a lot of Czechs here?

No, they probably go to the Salvation Army. There are old bills in an old drawer that are sold for collectors, they're worth absolutely nothing. So they fucking go there and buy two or three tattered old Czech bills for fifty Swiss centimes, to try to pass them off to us as dollars or something. There was one, on a Saturday, he rang the bell and I closed the door immediately. And he was the one who put his foot in the jamb, I had to give him a big punch in the stomach, he almost broke his face in the stairway, I screamed at him, you see, women have muscles, I mean, you know, it's a battle. It's a fight.

Why did you refuse this one?

He never has a sou! Or he takes out forty francs instead of fifty. He's pissed off the whole neighborhood. Ida had already told me, you should never take him.

Ida?

Yes, a woman who's going to retire in three years because she's sixty already. She has no eyelashes, she has some kind of sickness in her eyes, but it doesn't matter, she has a fair amount of clients, even at sixty.

Was it a Spanish guy?

Yes, I think he was Spanish. I think they enjoy fucking with us. You see, after all, we argued, kicked and punched, closed the door, they probably orgasm at that point, it doesn't seem possible otherwise, since they keep coming back to get insulted and beat up, so there must be something.

And the Arab guy you kicked out?

I love Arabs, as you know. But some of them aren't very nice. I mean, it depends which ones. Maybe it's that from one humiliation to the next, they want to get some revenge for once, I mean, they get their revenge in little pieces. First, I did it for him for a hundred French francs, he was still acting correct, let's say. A bit brutal, a little annoying, a little frustrating, a little too long, but basically correct. But by the end he wasn't happy, he wanted to do it twice for the same price, he had to be flipped back and forth in all directions like a crêpe. You know when you're on the bed here, you have to show them some ass, but very quickly, because otherwise they'll want to do everything from behind. I mean come on! And then, you have no idea how miserable it is. These guys, they think they're on a ladder, they try to climb and climb, you have to raise your ass to the ceiling, I mean it's horrifying. It's too awful. And then afterwards, when they pull out, I'm always afraid a lake will pour out, so you have to change the sheets again... So this Arab, to finish the story, he was annoying me so much that I didn't want to have him back. But he came back anyway. So he was here at the door, he had rung the bell with a little bag in his hand. I said, come in, we're going to explain a few things to each other, because I don't want to see you anymore, but I want to tell you why. So he came in, he was delighted, charmed. He thought that that was it, I was going to take him back. A tall Arab, dry and bony. Oh, he must have been around 35. Aggressive, you know. Sure of himself. Macho. So he put his bag here. And then he got ready to take his clothes off, I said no. We're gonna talk first, I said I don't want you anymore because you're not correct. What do you mean not correct! Yes, you have no respect for women. He was surprised, because no woman had ever told him that. I said yes, not only do you have no respect for women, but in your country, Algeria, women are dogs. They're nothing. But this is not Algeria, and women must be respected. But I respect them. I said no, no, it's not true. You do not respect them. This is why I don't want you anymore. So he said ok, but do you like men? I said what? I can't look at them! I can't stand to look at them anymore. I can't stand men anymore, I hate them. So he was stuck, because over there, you know, these handsome guys, they're used to having everyone at their feet, loving them, thinking they're so gorgeous, wanting them.

And he was handsome?

Not too ugly. But he thought he was so great.

You didn't like him?

No. I mean, I would have liked him if he had been nice. Oh, do you need money? I said what money. I have as much as I want. And anyway I don't care, I don't need money. What I want is to be left in peace. I want peace. So then he couldn't talk anymore. It was too much. He picked up his bag and left. Without telling a bunch of stories. You know, some of them turn bad. I shocked him, he got the hell out of here. But he started trying to come over again. But I wouldn't explain anything anymore, just close the door and be done with it.

Have you ever been attacked by an Arab?

Oh! Almost. It depends if they've been drinking. When an Arab's been drinking, he'll get hard less easily. And this already makes him unpleasant, because he gets frustrated. And if you're a little brusque with him on top of that or if you're not accommodating enough, that's it! There was one, one time, who was so exasperating, he just couldn't get hard. So I said listen, there's no point in drinking that much and then coming here. Always Saturday, naturally. Because you can see perfectly well it doesn't work. Yes it does, yes it does, it works great. I said but come on, look at yourself, you've got nothing! Yes yes, it's gonna come, it's ok, it's ok. So I said look, I've had enough. I saw that there was a red glimmer lighting up in his eyes, and then that he'd stiffened like that, I said, this is gonna get ruined. So I became very sweet again, very patient, very kind, even though I'd really had enough. And I definitely avoided something there. Recently a girl got stabbed by a Turk. I have Turks over every weekend. Sometimes ten of them. They've never done a single thing to me. They're angels. First of all, I charge them a hundred French francs. And then when they take me in their arms, I let myself be taken, when they kiss me on the cheek I let them, if they want to kiss me on the mouth, I close it a little, you see, I do the strict minimum, but still, I'm human. If they want me to suck their cock, I suck it, if they don't want it, because there's a Muslim taboo, I don't suck it, I adapt. So after, they thank me with tears in their eyes, they say, "You nice, madame, why you so nice?" Come on, I say, it's normal! But there are girls, you know, first they're wearing motorcycle jackets, those're expensive, and then they don't know how to maneuver with the Turks. They tell them, hurry up, you're getting on my nerves. And then, give me a hundred more francs. So this one Turk, apparently he couldn't ejaculate. That would have surprised me, I've had Turks drunk out of their minds, they always come. It happened at Hotel Till, next door. She asked him for two hundred Swiss francs, some poor laborer, that shows she had no class, to ask him for two hundred Swiss francs.

That's five hundred French francs.

Apparently he worked in Switzerland, but still. That's an enormous sum. She's some little nana, twenty-five years old, apparently. So it didn't work. They both put their clothes back on, and at that moment the Turk, all of a sudden it went to his head, he must have said to himself, shit, two hundred Swiss francs for nothing, he came at her with a knife, she put her arm up, she took it all in her arm, but they had to operate on her, put her to sleep in the hospital, it was serious. Her arm was more or less paralyzed for a year. But me, even with Spanish guys, drunk off their asses, who can't come, and there's nothing worse than a Spanish guy who can't come, they get insanely furious, I mean, look. I get them to get dressed, I insult them, I yell at them until they get dressed and I kick them the fuck out the door. They've never done something like that to me, not even slapped me, nothing. Because I show that I'm not afraid. The other day, it wasn't longer ago than Saturday, this annoying little Spanish guy came by. You're sure you haven't had too much to drink? No, no, no. They've never had anything to drink but they can't even stand up. I said, listen, if you've been drinking, it's not gonna work for me, understand? Ok, then give me the money. If you don't pay, you're out of here. If you don't wanna leave I'll break your face. I'm not afraid. So in the end, they respect me. You see. You have to mix patience, kindness, and rage. You have to make an impression on them.

The pearl you have around your neck, a client gave that to you, I think.

A lovely client, Spanish. But he's a cultivated gentleman. Not a laborer. He always brings me jewelry from Spain, he calls me on my birthday. It's a fake pearl, but it's more beautiful than real ones.

(Laughter.) *And the Spanish guy in the coma, what's that about?*

Oh! Drunk off his ass, he couldn't stand up! He wanted to come back last night, I'm telling you, this guy. He's a tiny little Spaniard. I'm telling you, they're miniscule, these poor Spanish guys. I think they could never eat enough back home, so they never grew. You know, a man who's short is already aggressive, because he feels smaller than other people. So they drink all day Saturday. They show up Saturday night totally wasted. They've been drinking because they're depressed, because they're too short, because nobody likes them, because they're alone, and they show up here, they can't stand up. They try to act like it's nothing. But I couldn't see right away this tiny Spaniard was trashed, he showed up sliding against the walls trying to act like he could walk straight. I didn't realize it right away. But on the bed he weighed three tons, he was like this, on me, I said what's wrong with this guy? Oh la la. He couldn't even hold himself up on me, he let himself slide like a lead brick. Naturally he didn't get hard, didn't ejaculate, I mean it was a whole story, I did my best. But in the end, I got him to come, it was a miracle, but because he was totally exhausted, he completely collapsed in the hallway. Yes. Alcohol coma. Something I'd never seen. He was snoring. He was totally snoring. So because he'd gone into a coma on me, I pushed him out with all my strength. I said no way, this is not possible. A Sunday afternoon! I'm gonna be stuck here all day with a Spanish guy in a coma. I went insane I was so mad, so I insulted him. Piece of shit! Why the fuck did you come here, get up you bastard, I yelled and yelled. I'd put his socks, his underwear, his undershirt, his pants back on, but I couldn't close them. And then his shirt, we can't even talk about it. I mean, he was like glued to my carpet with araldite.

Araldite?

It's a glue that's so strong that you can't ever unstick it, they glue boats with it. I was so mad I was insane, I was pacing like a tiger in my kitchen, I washed up, dried off, got dressed, and then I said, I have to get rid of this Spaniard, I can't drag him, impossible, too heavy. So I called a girlfriend of mine, American, a lady who's sixty years old already. I said, you know, June, I'm desperate, I've got a Spaniard in a coma at my place, I don't know what to do. So she sent me her fourteen-year-old daughter with a Spanish friend of hers, a young guy, pretty strong. It was just in time. The three of us managed to pick up this comatose heap, to get it dressed, and finally, to get it to stand up. It wasn't easy. All of a sudden it opened an eye, and I heard psffff! psfff! Like it was nothing. I said, what? So you've been drinking after all? I didn't have anything to drink, he said. I mean, come on! I opened the door and right away he fell halfway back into his coma. We had to catch him so he wouldn't fall down the stairs or break a leg or something. So we said, where are we gonna put him now, we can't leave him in the stairwell, so we ask him where're you going? Oh! I don't know! But where do you live? I don't know. Where do you wanna go? To the bistro. Fine, I said, deposit this shit in the nearest bistro, I never want to see it again. Oh! He came back six times. And I have no memory. But this guy, I'd photocopied him into my brain. Every time he rang the bell, I opened, I said, "What? I don't wanna see you ever again." So he went back downstairs, tail between his legs. He came back three, four days later, ringing the bell, he had such a heart-breaking look on his face, I said no, I don't have the heart, I have to give him one more chance. So I let him in, listen to this, it's extraordinary. He came in walking on eggshells, I said, ok, we'll see. You haven't been drinking? Oh no! We'll see. I'll give you one chance. So he took his clothes off, he had a smile, it was like he'd arrived in Paradise. He gave me ten francs extra. When he handed me the fifty franc bill, I saw that there was a ten franc bill folded up inside. I said, what's this? I wanted to give it back to him, but he said no, no. It's for you, because you let me back in. He made love. He was a little slow, he'd definitely had a cocktail, but not too much. After, he offered me cigarettes, he thanked me for my kindness, you see what I mean. After all, they're horribly lonely. Nobody wants them. Girls are rude to them, they don't have wives, fiancées, they have nothing, they're sick of jacking off all year.

A month ago, there was a wave of Spanish guys, because they arrive at the train station; they show up here suitcase in hand. I just got back from Spain, on vacation. They're all tan, they ejaculate much faster because they've been deprived. It's mysterious. I don't know how these guys manage to make love, they show up on their way home from the station, they're barely off the train and they show up at your place, they put down their suitcase, get naked, and bam! It's extraordinary! And they come see you too when they're about to get on the train. Oh! I'm in a rush, I'm going on vacation. They come so fast, and they say, "You're not sick? You sure, sure, because I'm going to my family in Spain. To my wife's. I can't bring her back something." It's touching. A lot of them say to me, you know, I'm faithful to you because as soon as I find a woman who pleases me I stay with her, I don't want to change.

There are Spanish guys I've known for four years now. There's one, at first he barely dared to get undressed, and now he comes over and asks if he can keep my garter belt, my bra, some shoes or boots, in front of the mirror we do a whole show, he really gets his pleasure visually, and in his brain. But before, it was a totally shameful sexuality, you see, condemned by the Catholic church. But the Spanish guy who gave me this pearl, he told me that in Spain, in certain villages and even in cities, a woman, when her husband fucks her, the light has to be off, the woman has to be in some kind of nightshirt she's not allowed to take off, I mean, there are no flourishes, no caresses, before or after. They penetrate the woman, they make a baby while thinking of Jesus.

Do they bring their friends to you?

Sometimes they come two at a time. And they bring a third who wouldn't dare come alone because he just got off the train, he's new to this country, he doesn't know anyone, Swiss women kind of scare him. I mean, there are aggressive girls here. How many times has a Spanish guy told me, look, I have three friends in the street, I'm gonna send them to you, you'll be nice to them? Like with me! Nice, huh? I'm counting on you. I say of course, as usual. You see the confidence of these people, they bring me their friends. I refuse the young guys who come ringing, but when it's an old Spanish guy, another client who brings him, I can't refuse. I can't. It can't have been more than the day before yesterday, a gorgeous young Spaniard came over, a gypsy. A real gypsy, and too beautiful. Much too beautiful to be a client. I had to take him. He'd been brought by another guy. That's when you realize that they must live in a profound loneliness, because to be that handsome, that young, and to be so alone! Obviously they don't know French, there's the language barrier, so they're forced to come to prostitutes. Forced. And you can't even exchange a few words with them because they don't understand anything. It's all by gestures, looks, kisses, caresses. In a way that's not too bad... *(Laughter.)*

Are there Swiss men who come in groups?

Yes. It's happened. But you have no idea how annoying it is. They show up, a group of four or five. They've just been in a bar, they've had a drink, and they show up here.

What was it like the last time?

So there were two here and two here, another one in the kitchen, I had to wash them all...

How old were they?

Oh, they must have been 30, 40 years old. So they'd had a drink to give themselves some courage. They showed up here. You see, Solange, she's nice… I was a little surprised, but I mean, you get to a point where nothing can really surprise you. So I let them in, I said, listen, it's gonna be a hundred francs each, because for this kind of job you have to pay extra. So fine, I have to wash them, soap them, rinse them, dry them, then I have to suck one while the other ones masturbate or just watch, or there's one who's timid, he's staring, you know what I mean. One's hard, so he wants to make love, the other ones watch to encourage themselves. Then one laughs, the other one goes soft, I mean, these things never end.

How long does it last?

Oh! Hours. There's always one who can't make it to the end. The others, they manage, but there's always one who doesn't, while the others are all happy, they say, see, you can't do it. The guy who gets hard first and stays hard the best will ejaculate first. You have to serve, like ping-pong or a hockey match, you have to serve, you know…

Do they yell a lot or are they totally silent?

All they do is make fun of each other, it's awful!

You weren't afraid that they'd gang up on you, rape you?

No! You don't realize, since they can't get hard by themselves, they're hoping it'll give them courage to be in a group and then as soon as one of them's hard, the other ones say, well I'm gonna try to get there too. It's just competition among boys. It's very particular.

In truth, they wouldn't even need women. But you're there as an alibi. It's like groups of grammar school kids jacking off together in a bathroom.

You've had them over more than once, these four or five guys?

Oh! Twice.

Did you put them in the black book?

No.

Why?

Well, they didn't call again after that.

They came over just like that?

Yeah, like that, improvised, at 2 or 3 in the morning. I was about to go to bed. So already, you're exhausted, and this herd descends on you, and then it lasts an hour, two hours, three hours, until the last one finally ejaculates, hiding from the others. I mean, honestly. Things like this just kill you, they wear you to the bone! *(Laughter.)*

And the English guy. The one you had last week?

Oh, that was a glorious rescue! You should have seen how happy he was afterward. We drank a whiskey to celebrate, it was fabulous. So, some people I didn't know spoke to a friend of mine out of concern for a friend of theirs, they said look, we have a friend who's horribly depressed. He's on the brink of suicide. In fact he's had one suicide attempt, he can't take it anymore, he's falling into another depression, he's gonna come to Geneva to find a psychiatrist. So might there be a way for us to send him to a compassionate woman beforehand? Because he's tried going to prostitutes before, and it hasn't worked.

Where was he from?

London. He was 34 years old. He'd never been able to make love to a woman. Can you imagine the anguish of a 34-year-old guy who wants to make love and can't? You know me well, naturally I accepted him right away. The doorbell rang. I had to talk in English. I had him come in, a bearded guy, kind of a redhead, with blue eyes. Totally charming, cultivated, friendly, really nothing of the obsessive about him, nothing like a mental patient, not macho at all. A completely normal man. So he was standing right here, he didn't move. I said to myself, ok, I guess he is a little touched. I said, OK, make yourself comfortable, make yourself at home, put your clothes down here. He got undressed very naturally, and I did the same. I brought him into the kitchen. I said, is it alright for you to give me a hundred francs, will you agree to that. Because they'd told me he had money. I don't want to rob people, but I don't want to fuck for nothing either. He gave me the hundred francs very politely. I put them in my bag, I washed this gentleman, I dried him off, he came back over here, he wasn't moving, I said: lie down and relax, make yourself at home. Lie down here, that's right, just make yourself comfortable. I said to myself, there's no need to put him in front of the mirror to do anything fancy; he's already blocked, it's better to keep it simple. Because afterwards, they'll say, she's insane, she's hysterical, she wants to suck my cock in front of a mirror, what the fuck is that! Him, what he wanted was just to manage to make love, that's all. He didn't need a bunch of cinema.

Well?

Well alright, he was on the bed, lying down, he wasn't moving. I sat down next to him, I took his cock, I started to suck it discreetly, caressing his balls a little, his thighs, all over. And he got hard. I said to myself, this isn't normal, because a guy who's never made love, I thought he was thirty, he was thirty-four, if he gets hard this fast, something's fishy. So I asked him, Have you ever made love to a woman? He said, yeah, yeah, I've gone out with women, but I've never made love. "Oh! No problem."[1] There's nothing difficult about it, it'll come on its own. "Take it easy." Don't worry! I was still sucking and he had a good hard-on, and I said to myself after a while, he can't have come here to ejaculate in my mouth, because if that's all he wanted he would have found a way to do that elsewhere. What he wants is definitely to make love, to really make love, the way it's written in the Bible. So after a while I said, ok, you can get on me, and he said OK. I took the pillows off, I lay down.

Did he kiss you?

Yes. He kissed me on the mouth and inside too, and I let him do it, I figured it was doing him good. Had to reassure him at all costs. But after a while I realized I was waiting for him, I said to myself, this guy has a problem, I haven't figured out what it is yet, but I know I'll find out soon enough. I found out! He was on top of me, he'd penetrated me with his cock and he was fucking, but after a while, all of a sudden, I noticed he became hesitant and sad, he said, "Oh! I must relax!" And he'd gone completely soft. But I said to myself, now my sweetie, you're gonna make it! Because I didn't have all night, I had to go to the post office to send some urgent documents. The post office closes at quarter to eleven and it was already ten at night, so we had to get going. I said, "Oh! No problem." And I said to myself, this poor guy,

---

1. In English in the original.

if at age thirty he hasn't been able to make love, he must have still managed to jack off. So he must have always had the contact of his own hand. So, since I'm always a little crafty, I had him lie down like this, and I slid my hand over the base of his cock, he was still inside, maybe a quarter of his cock was still inside, three quarters outside, so I held it very firmly in my hand. And since he had the reassuring feeling of a hand squeezing his cock, well, he got hard again. So I squeezed, I held on, I set it in motion without letting go, the head was still inside me. I said let's hope. After a little bit it was hard again, pretty hard. So I said I better not let go now. So I kissed him, I stroked his back, I put my feet on his ass, I gave him a few little kicks, he started to laugh, I said great, good sign! I stopped the little kicks, but I squeezed him with my thighs, my feet, my knees. And I scratched his back a little, figuring that if he was a little bit masochist that might activate him a little. And right away I felt it, because you feel everything, I felt his cock swelling from below, that means that the sperm was hardening it. It was climbing. Oh la la! As long as it goes all the way up. So I did the maximum, it's like in an orchestra, you know, when you attack the finale and the guy, without wanting to, it happened in spite of him, it was swelling, the sperm went higher, higher, higher, and he ejaculated for the first time in his life, thirty-four years old, in a woman's vagina. I thought he would die, he was like, Ah, ah ah! I said my god, *quelle horreur*! He's gonna die on my bed. He was overwhelmed. I've rarely seen this. When they ejaculate at thirty, at forty for the first time in their life, it's like they're gonna die. It's like a death. They stay like that, they don't move. They don't talk, they don't breathe. I was stroking his back, I said, it's great, it happened! And he said, *Oh yes!* He couldn't even talk, poor thing. For the first time in his life. I said, oh, it's so good. This is great, just relax, and I left him there. I went to bathe and then I said, do you wanna drink a little whiskey? *Oh yes!* So I brought whiskey, water, ice, and we celebrated. He was so happy. And afterwards, he wanted to continue. Because this British guy, in my opinion, is extremely gifted for love, he'd just never been able to express it.

Why gifted for love?

Because he's an enthusiast. About a woman's body. He wanted to do everything at once. He said, can I put my finger inside. I said, I just finished bathing. It wasn't that, but I had to get to the post office, but otherwise yes, otherwise I would have said, you can give me a little present and we'll stay a little longer. He could have done everything, touched everything, felt everything. But the post office was gonna close. I had to... hurry him along a little, but I didn't want to. He said, can I come over again, another time? I said listen, the best thing for you to do would be to fall in love with a nice woman, and then you'll make love with her, for love. That's really the best thing that could happen to you.

And the last time you had love, it was the Berber?

Oh! Yes, but that's still going on, really. Listen, I haven't heard from him, he's probably in prison. Every winter he goes to prison, because he doesn't know where else to go. So he goes on a huge bender, wrecks a bar, beats up two or three tourists, so he winds up in the can, that way at least he's warm, fed, housed for the winter.

How did you meet him?

Well, I met him over time. Because I met him at a big party, in '71, I think... given by an insane guy from Berne, thanks to the alcoholic lover I had at the time. I didn't keep him long. He drank so much he couldn't get hard, and anyway, I didn't love him. So we were in Lausanne, in a huge fiesta. We were dancing, drunk off our asses, and all of a sudden the guy from Berne disappeared. Afterward, I received a letter from a prison in Berne, Thorberg, it's one of the worst penitentiaries in Switzerland. "Dear Grisélidis, I heard a radio show with you in it, so I'm writing to you, I'm in prison." It made my heart sore, so I answered this guy I'd only seen one time at a party, I wrote, don't worry, my friend, it'll pass, things will go better for you. And after a few letters, he wrote, "I'm not alone in my cell, there's a Berber here with me, it'll be his birthday soon, nobody cares, he's very unhappy. Could you send him a birthday package with some coffee, tobacco, and don't forget a postcard." So I bought a pretty postcard, the Berber probably still has it, and I wrote, "Brother, don't worry, I'm thinking of you, it will pass, happy birthday." It was the beginning of a correspondence, and eventually we were writing each other every day no matter what. Love letters. We'd never seen each other! So he made suicide attempts, had nervous breakdowns, attacked his guards, wrecked his cell, so that they'd transport him to French Switzerland. Finally, he managed to get himself transplanted to the countryside, to Bochuz, and I went to see this Berber every two weeks by train, we'd spend a half hour, forty-five minutes in a visiting room in front of cops. That's how we got to know each other. And then afterwards, we wanted to get married.

But the first time you saw him?

Oh! I was blown away! You know, I didn't know what I was going to see. And then, one of my snakes had lost an eye. I should have listened, because you see, every time my snakes lose their eyes, that means a great misfortune is gonna befall me.

And that very day one of my snakes had lost an eye. Well I didn't listen to the snake, I said shit, I don't care. And I went to meet the Berber in prison. That was the beginning of nine years of sorrow.

But nine years of sorrow and nine years of passion.

Yeah, yes, of course. But you know, when you're with a Berber who's an alcoholic, homosexual, gigolo, thief, prostitute, and totally violent, and when he's been drinking and he breaks your face and nearly kills you three times a week, well, it's hard!

What did he look like?

Oh! He was fairly short. Like a guy who's a little too short, and that makes him mean. There's some kind of horrible morgue at the core of him all the time, you know, he'd been humiliated, beaten, since he was little. So obviously he gets his revenge wherever he can. In general, these kinds of guys avenge themselves if possible on the woman who loves them. Because they know very well she won't go to the cops. She'll pay for everything, she'll sob, and then afterward they'll make up on the pillow.

Was he handsome?

Oh yes! Of course. I have the photo in my bag. I didn't show you the most recent one?

No.

I still have it in my bag. Despite everything! Because he drove me insane, but love is love... Good lord, where is it? Here it is! It's the last time I saw him, in February '78, we'd made peace. "Long live our love! Cafe de la Paix. February 1978. Grisélidis." It was in Tunis. He'd been deported to Tunisia, he couldn't come back to Europe. See, he'd grown a mustache.

Yes!

Oh, poor Berber! In the end, I sort of gave up, it's tiring getting yourself killed all the time. It was costing me too much, I always had to send him money and he got drunk on it. They were cursed years. Cursed to the end, I'm not suicidal enough, I guess, to want to suffer that kind of passion to the point of complete destruction. I mean, from the moment I let it drop I came back to life. Whereas before I was always at zero, in pieces, you know, I was crushed, I cried night and day, I ended up committing suicide for him. I woke up in a hospital in Paris, Lannec hospital, covered in tubes, tubes on my hands and feet and a tube in my throat they later pulled out, they had to operate on my vocal cords, because I hadn't been able to speak for months, I mean, it was horrific. I almost died.

You'd taken pills?

The Berber's sleeping pills.

But why did you want to kill yourself?

I couldn't take it anymore. Listen, after everything he'd done to me, he wanted to leave me to live with Loulou, one of his tricks. That was too much. And he was the one who told me to die. He wanted to leave me, but I was at the end of my strength. I said, if you leave me then there's nothing left for me, I'll die. He said fine, then die already! I said oh, die already, fine, I'll die. There! I tried and death wanted nothing to do with me. You don't always get what you want. So now I've decided to forget him.

How many suicide attempts have you made?

Oh la la! Lots of times… Let's see, once… I was seventeen, it didn't work. Yeah, I must have had three or four. But you know, it's pointless, because you fail… In general, it's always from misery in love. Oh, yes, my god!… The most spectacular ones were for misery in love, at least, I mean I had a huge hole in one lung, and I still managed to give birth to my fourth child. I mean, it happened a lot. I was completely at the end of my strength. And then a lover left me, he said take your things and go.

Who was it?

Huh? After giving birth, with a huge hole in one lung? Well, it was one of my lovers, I loved him a lot. A musician.

What was his name?

His name was Gilbert. He's on a poster over here. So you see…

But why was he spectacular, how did it work with you?

It was totally spectacular, in many ways, because you see, he's an old poet, I mean, he wasn't all that old, a fat poet who's since died, who saved me. Claude Aubert. He owed me ten Swiss francs, and on that particular day, he said to himself, I better go give her back her ten francs. And then he bought me a drink. He was always welcome here. So he told me that afterward, he'd come up the stairs, he heard music, and there was a whole family of cats asleep on the bed next to me, and I was yellow as a quince. There was a record spinning. I'd fainted.

Had you taken barbiturates?

Yes, a lot of barbiturates. A whole tube. So the poet, he ran out yelling, he spun around the courtyard like a madman calling for help. Apparently an ambulance showed up, and then I had to go to a window to pay two and a half francs for the price of transport. And I got yelled at. The cop in the window said, do you know, madame, it's an offence, you should not commit suicide. So you owe two and a half francs for the ambulance. And then you'd better not do it again, because next time there'll be a fine.

(Laughter.) *But why did you have a huge hole in one lung?*

Because I had goddamn tuberculosis! But I got cured later. I didn't know I had it. I found out that a bunch of women had tuberculosis, we found ourselves in a sanatorium, and there were dozens, I mean, they'd all been in depression. There were some who'd smashed all their dishes in their husbands' face, others who'd try to jump out the window, some had tried suicide like me, I mean, it was despair. Tuberculosis depresses you, it pushes you to suicide and despair. It also pushes a lot of people to make love.

Really?

Yes. Any tubercular will tell you. On one hand they're thinking of death, and on the other all they can think of is fucking. Maybe that makes sense, who knows…

Do girls sometimes die there?

Yes, from overdosing or suicide. There's one prostitute I liked so much, everyone loved her, her name was Elisabeth, we called her Lili, and not only was her family constantly driving her to suicide, to the point where she actually did it, but they'd even tried to hide her death, they'd taken their heartless cruelty to the point of preventing people from saying goodbye to her in the morgue. I'd started collecting money to pay for flowers, but I had to give all the money back, because the family said we couldn't even see her in the morgue, and then they immediately had her burnt and they brought the ashes into German Switzerland so that no one would see them, so that we couldn't even say goodbye to her. Lili, she had a horrific death. She'd tried to kill herself I don't know how many times, she was always either entering or coming out of the psychiatric clinic.

How did she kill herself?

She always did it with sleeping pills. She was drunk on medication, and I said to her, Lili, you can't go on like this, you should go to the countryside, to Appenzell, there are doctors there with plant-based medicines, they could get you back on your feet. Put you back together, like new. Regenerate the organism, because there's no point eating Valium and sleeping pills, bullshit to wake up or fall asleep, it completely fucks you up. It totally intoxicates you. Nothing works in your body anymore, and then you're depressed all year round, you can't sleep, you can't digest anything, you can't do anything anymore you're so trashed on chemical bullshit. So poor Lili, she couldn't get out of anything anymore. And in the end, she killed herself, but I don't know if I should say this, I mean, I heard that since she couldn't manage it on her own, she'd gotten someone to put a plastic bag over her head, they found her like that, a plastic bag tied around her neck so she'd suffocate, so she wouldn't wake up. You can't do that on your own. She must have paid someone she was so sick of it all… failing her suicides.

What's changed for you in ten years, in fifteen years, with clients?

I have regulars who've been coming for fifteen years. Since I quit prostitution for seven years and four months, I've found some old regulars who looked for me all over the place for seven years and four months, they found me, they come back from time to time. It's an amazing fidelity.

You have a fifteen-year client?

Oh! Yes. Paul. He calls me the goddess of love.

How old is he, Paul?

Oh, between fifty and sixty... And then Jean... The one who kind of looks like a gangster, Jean... Hang on, we'll find him... Jean... Here, this black book, it started.... But I didn't put the date? When was it? In '77, it's '81 now, that makes four years. So here, I've written Jean. Longtime client of seven years.

That makes eleven years now.

You see... "Enormous, distinguished gangster-from-the-Midi type, suck, finger in his ass, comes in mouth 100 F." Well, I still have him, he comes back regularly. He comes every two weeks, more or less. He likes me a lot. I try to make it new a little, every time. Refresh things. He's always glad; me too.

In your way of doing things, what has changed, do you feel more tender? Stronger? Tougher?

Well, I feel a lot more complicit.

You love them a little?

Well, I do my best. I know that if a man has a sensitive area, if it takes him so much time, ten minutes, a half hour, an hour, to get to the point of coming, I don't want to disappoint him. I give what he asks of me. Here, "Paul, client of 7 years, around 50. (Well, now he's fifty-four.) Nice, sentimental, suck, fuck, 100 F. Calls me the goddess of love." Well, he comes back regularly and calls me up, he says, I must see you immediately. It's wonderful!

You feel complicit because they're kind of your age?

No. I feel complicit because it's been ten or eleven years they've required my services. So…

But you would never call them?

Come on, I don't know where they are. I don't know their names. I don't have their phone numbers.

That doesn't bother you?

No, quite the opposite. This way, we stay very free. Them, they call me when they need to see me. And the rest of the time they leave me in peace. I never call them. Because I don't have their number, I don't even know their name. So it doesn't force me to give more than I can give. You see, they ask certain things of me, but not more.

But the fact that they're between forty-five and fifty-five years old, does that help you understand them better?

I know them so well I could have made them. I know all the little nuances, the subtleties, I know them as if I'd brought them into the world. And that must be why they come to me. Any old whore…

You can say to yourself that you're old, old, but with a few special nuances, after age forty-five, fifty. I went to the funeral of an old whore, seventy-nine years old and she still had her regulars coming to see her. They have to come back to us, because we know every detail of their orgasms, their little caprices, their little weaknesses and strengths. We know all of it. I mean, where do you expect them to go? They'll be disappointed anywhere else. Except for with us, because we know them like the back of our hand. As soon as they get in the door, it's like we'd made them ourselves. We know all the right things to say, all the gestures, there're no surprises, know what I mean. It's something that's been set up for ten, fifteen years. You can't make a mistake.

Like an old couple?

Yes, it's even better than an old couple, because they don't expect us to orgasm with them. So that's one less annoyance. You see, it's one less unknown. Because a woman who's married to a man, she's been making him come a long time, but once in a while she wants a little pleasure too. So because most women are frigid, or complicated, I mean, they have problems, it's problematic for husbands, it requires a huge amount of work for them, they're not always on the level. It's not easy to make a frigid woman come. We were all frigid once, so I know what I'm talking about. So when you go to an old whore who's like an old friend, an old mama, an old sister, an old cousin, well, you don't have any problems. Because the most you're gonna ask this old whore is to fake an orgasm once in a while, I mean, Jean said to me, all I ask is that someone have the kindness to do a tiny bit of cinema for me, nothing more. Some of them don't even bother giving me a tiny bit of cinema, it's like they don't give a fuck about me.

You told me earlier, I'm feeling kind of tired, but it's better in the morning. Do you feel your age?

Oh! I don't let myself get stuck by age, I resist it! I fuck with it, huh, aging! You understand what I'm saying, it costs a lot, being old!

You feel well in the morning?

I never feel totally well, but I fight it. Aging is a usury of your organs, your body, your brain, your ass, your stomach, your liver, your intestines, it's just usury. Everyday you have to tell yourself, I'm gonna T.K.O. this little bit of usury. Because my stomach, it fucks me over, my intestines don't wanna work, I have pains here, and here, my teeth are no good, my ass is no good, so you have to fight constantly, fight to keep afloat, to stay at the surface. When you're young you don't need to give a shit, everything works on its own. And then later it works worse and worse. I don't want to let myself get taken over, not by this usury of my organs, or by age, or exhaustion, or morale, I mean, not by any weaknesses, I want to resist, keep on resisting. So my youth means renewing myself every day, every day saying fuck you to everything that goes wrong. Before I didn't need to bother, but now I'm extremely conscious that I have to say fuck you to everything, because otherwise those are the things that T.K.O. you.

You think you'll die of this?

What? Die doing a client? More likely it's the client who'll die, if you wanna know. They're the ones who are deficient, because the poor things, listen, how many old guys do I have coming to me, they say to me, you don't realize, you're giving me back myself at twenty. It's thanks to you I can still make love. The doctor tells me to go to you and everything. It's more likely them who die on us. We don't have time to die, we're too busy bringing life to them. You understand, we don't have a single minute to die. You have to be here and help these wretches not die on the spot.

You've never been to a client's funeral?

No! Not a client's. I've been to the funerals of certain old whores, but clients, them, they don't give their last names, they don't announce to us the date of their death, but those dates are inscribed on their faces and in their balls, we're not totally sure of the exact date it's gonna happen, but... And anyway, all that's taken care of by their wife, their mother-in-law, their children, their concierge, all that's none of our business.

How do you like to dress?

Oh! You know, since I'll be fifty-two in August, now I don't give a shit how old I am anymore, so I bought myself the kind of clothes that would have caused a scandal when I was twenty, so fine, let them cause a scandal when I'm fifty.

Like what?

I have sexy whore clothes! Fabulous! Tiny fur shorts with fur vests, and I walk the sidewalk half naked, but there are women who start bitching, they say "Come on, at her age!" And it bothers them, because they have to say to themselves: after all, she doesn't look too bad!... I also have a little faux panther skirt, transparent blouses, a faux lizard dress, I mean, I have everything.

What's your favorite color?

Black, and animal skins, even artificial, as long as they look a little fake, a bit...

Barbaric?

Yeah, a little barbaric... Wild. Yeah, wild. You know? Primitive, the jungle, I eat you or you eat me, I mean, brutal relationships.... Not sophisticated, not evolved, you know, not... How should I say this? I want to look kind of... prehistoric. Yeah, you know? I want it to look prehistoric. Like we're in the caves, with the desire either to devour or be devoured at the same time. One after the other, or both at the same time. Because that's what love is, like, a predator's meal.

When was the last time you were jealous?

Oh! You know, it's always my Berber. So, I thought he was making me jealous on purpose so I'd fall in love. But that was a miscalculation on his part, because I was in love anyway, but he didn't feel very sure of my love, and anyway, he could never feel very sure of anything his whole life. So he tried to make me jealous, he'd say, I'm going to Pigalle, I'm gonna get wasted, there are whores up there who let me stay the whole night, they buy my drinks, kiss me on the mouth, let me sleep in their beds. All that sounds like fun to me, but it still caused me some pain anyway, so I said fine, if he's so happy, he better stay there! Why does he come back to me to tell me about it, just to make me suffer?

You don't like that?

Not so much. I didn't understand exactly what he was trying to get. Either to disgust me, or to get rid of me like dead weight, or to try to incite me to love him even more. But he made a mistake. Because I adore those Pigalle whores! So if the Berber was so happy with them, I mean, I'd give him to them gladly to make them all happy!

And when he went out with tricks?

Oh, well that was calculated, he'd say to me, you know, I'm going to Loulou's, I'm going to so-and-so's, he gives me fifty francs a day, he gives me a hundred francs a day. I can take a bath. Back then I had a studio, I didn't have a shower. It was kind of facile of him. He'd say, he gives me pocket money, I can take a bath, there's a bed, a big conjugal bed, there's food in the refrigerator, cigarettes, everything I want, there's a television. So I said to myself, this is just a song and dance so I'll give him more. I thought it was sordid.

Was he kind of a pimp?

Yeah, a pimp without really being one. When he was a kid he had nothing, and he just always wanted more and more.

But you love him?

I loved him because he wrote me a love letter from prison. And since I needed love myself, it was kind of miraculous that a man in prison who had never seen me would love me like that. I understood pretty well why. I understood later.

It was a beautiful letter?

Oh yes! They were sublime letters. And they were totally sincere. And I think he still loves me in his way. He wants to make me pay for everything he ever lacked, he wants me to pay for the lack of love from his mother, the bullshit cops in Tunisia, he wants to make me pay for all the injustices he suffered in Europe… But in the meantime I think he loves me truly. But it's a very dramatic love. It's a difficult love, because, no matter what you give it'll never be what he needs.

Have clients written to you?

Oh yes! I have letters in the other room, I have tons.

Love letters?

(Silence.) They're more like letters of gratitude…

Not love letters?

But then it wouldn't be a client. It would be a man in love. But a man in love doesn't pay. It's free.

There isn't a client who could be loved? It's never happened?

Listen, I've fallen in love with clients two or three times. It was a total failure.

When was the last time? What was his name?

Oh, the last time… His name was Claude.

Claude?

Yes. I really loved this man.

A long time ago?

Oh yes! Years.

What was he like?

He was really handsome. He had a little beard. Of Czech origin, with green eyes, a wonderful man. He was younger than me. He was maybe eight or nine years younger than me at the time. And he even loved my kids. He was lovely. Only, you know, it couldn't work.

What was he doing in Switzerland?

Oh! Well he might still be here. He's married now.

Was he a laborer?

He was a typesetter. You see, he had his old mother who owned him on the one hand, and he'd been disappointed by young women, and I fell madly in love with him, I thought he was amazing.

Did he ever come here?

Oh! Not here, never. It was before, when I lived on the other side of the city.

And the first time?

The first time, I met him on the sidewalk, he came up to me as a client, and in the midst of doing him as a client I fell in love. I felt... Well I felt totally taken with this man. I'd fallen in love. And I'd let myself come for the first time. But he had problems, because let me tell you, a man who doesn't have problems is not gonna show up as a client anywhere.

So what was the problem?

The problem was in reality he hadn't fully passed the stage of being attached to his mother; he would have just liked to find a different mother.

Well? Was that you?

Yes. It was me. But at that time, I had to feed three of my four children, and I'd decided to work the sidewalk and to retire with a sum of money to write a book, it was in '68. So I was pursuing my goal. And since I wasn't finding a man who wanted to marry me, to insure me financially, well, I kept working the sidewalk.

Did he propose marriage to you?

Of course, but you know, deep inside, these men don't really want to get engaged. I would have had to remake myself into a factory worker or a salesgirl or model or something. But I was sick of all that.

But he came over often, he saw you outside of…

Yes, yes. We saw each other, we loved each other. We even took a trip together. To Bulgaria.

For a long time?

Oh! It lasted a good two, three weeks. But it's hard for a man to marry a prostitute. It doesn't make them happy that you get fucked all day or all night by other people. A man, when he loves a woman, he wants her for himself after all. I wouldn't want to share her with all those guys.

What did he say to you?

He didn't like it. He accepted the idea of it being temporary, short-lived, limited in time. But he didn't like it. And he didn't really want to deal with it in depth because I was older than he was. And I had been in love with someone else, he didn't like that.

You told him that?

Of course. I tell everything.

What was his name, the other one?

Oh! It was a very uncommon name, I don't know if I can say it... His name was Benedict... He's gotten married too, since then. You see, I lost all my lovers because they got married. But if they're happy with their wives, I don't regret anything.

How long did things last with Claude?

Oh! More than a year... But there was his old mother on one side and a young woman on the other...

Do you think you could have become a couple...

You know, it's extremely rare for something like that to work. And I am very independent. These guys, they want you at home, in their bed, but you have to exist for them above all. I don't want to exist solely for a man; that's way too limited in my opinion.

But you really loved him?

Yes. Yes, I adored him. I adored him... Well? Too bad, it got fucked up and that was it. He found a young woman, younger than me, who didn't whore herself out, from England. A young woman in love, wonderful. It's better that way; I'm glad about it. I'm not jealous. I'm glad he's well. I hope that it will work, that it will last forever. That they'll have children, that they'll be happy. That it'll be a balanced household, blossoming, marvelous, why not?

When do you think the rupture happened?

Oh! It happened when I got in touch with someone who used to be in love with me, he wouldn't accept it.

Benedict?

Yes.

Do you think that if you met Benedict or Claude again today, you'd be moved?

It's totally finished. Look, what's finished is finished. And even the Berber, I think it's finished... Even the Berber...

You can't imagine an impossible passion anymore? That could completely overwhelm you?

If you don't feel that you're bringing someone total happiness, it's better to stay away. Because it would only be little pieces and disillusions. But in my opinion, there has to be an ideal in common, because if a man only asks maternal and sexual security of you, well that's nice, but it's not enough. So in my opinion you have to see much further than that. You'd have to marry a nut, a surrealist poet, you'd have to love someone who's beyond the norm. Because love is not restrictive. If you get the impression that it's going to amputate you while restraining the other, it's not worth it.

Do you think you'll see him again?

Well, that's up to fate; I let myself be guided.

You'd give up everything?

I wouldn't give up anything if we got together to get a hold on things.

Would you give up prostitution?

But prostitution's to make a living. I don't have anything to live on. You know, when you have enormous telephone bills, rent, doctors, dentists, well, you have to find money. By being a prostitute I have a lot of liberty, because even if I only do one client a week, or a client every three days, I live. The second reason is that in my estimation prostitutes are extraordinary women, and as long as that's not a universally acknowledged thing, it's important to continue the struggle. And as an active prostitute I can continue this struggle much more effectively than if I said, listen, I was a prostitute back in the day, now I don't do it anymore. It doesn't have the same impact.

There haven't been any mustachioed little pimps seducing you?

Well come on, there are plenty of them! When I got here four years ago, there were gorgeous guys on motorcycles or motorbikes, it depended on the state of their fortunes, who'd come up to me, oh, hi, how's it going, I'd like to get to know you, I think you're beautiful. I said yes, ok, what the hell is this? There are even guys who were devious enough to come as clients. You see the ruse. Obviously these guys have problems like anyone else, I mean, they don't make it to the end. They blame alcohol, shyness, love, whatever. And all of a sudden… I'd hear these things, you know, I have debts, I have a thousand Swiss francs worth of debts, you know, I just got out of prison, I'm out of work. I'd say oh! My poor dear… So could you help me out a little bit? I said, well I'll think about it. These guys didn't come back a second time. Because I'm not that stupid. This is why I don't have pimps, because I wrapped them up and sent them out of here.

You've never fallen in love with a pimp?

Oh! I've fallen in love with men who'd hoped that they might become my pimp, but they were wrong. There was one I adored, loved…

What's his name?

He has two names, cause he has a fake one and a real one.

What's the fake one?

Matteo. There!

Was he Sicilian?

No. Oh! I guess he was sort of foreign. So I saw him again recently and I fell back in love, but I didn't show it. He came back here, he made eyes at me, tender, eyes deep as wells, all I had to do was bury myself in them. But I didn't bury myself.

He came back as a client?

Oh! Not at all! He came as a lover. But we didn't make love. Anyway, he's half impotent. He said, you see, I need you to loan me a hundred francs because I can't pay my rent. So I understood, since I know him well, I said, look, at my age, I'm not gonna go work the sidewalk for you. Go where you want, you'll work things out elsewhere, there's no lack of women out there, go borrow your hundred francs where you want, but not here. I was inflexible on this. I never saw him again. Couldn't somebody fall in love with me without asking me for money?!

When was the first time you did the work of a courtesan?

The very first time... Well, I was at a sanitarium in the mountains and I didn't have a cent, since we only got fifteen Swiss francs a month on Public Assistance, as pocket money. So you know...

How old were you?

Oh, I was thirty, yeah. It was 1959. They'd operated on my lung, from tuberculosis, and I was on medical Public Assistance. And all you see is fifteen Swiss francs a month for pocket money. I had been a model, so I'd never been a prostitute, and then what do you want, they operated on my lung, and I'd seen that there were injustices in the sanatorium, there were young women who were very sick and nobody wanted to operate on them because they didn't have any money, I mean look, it revolted me. So one night I escaped, I went out dancing, I wanted to have a good time, I escaped the sanatorium for some fun, and I met a man who offered me money to make love.

Where was this?

In Montana, that's about 1500 meters away, in the Valais canton.

And you accepted?

Look, I didn't have a franc in my pocket, and I was pretty good at fucking... I said, God, if it'll make him happy... He gave me a hundred francs, so I sucked his cock and that was it... I wrote a letter to a woman about it, I told her everything. Oh! I cried over it a little. I felt a little diminished, a little dirty... But in another way, I got over it very quickly by saying to myself, look, it was an accident in my life. An accident, it wasn't... It wasn't a contract. It was an accident.

In your opinion, are there guys who don't come see you anymore because they're afraid you'll talk?

I take enormous risks publishing all this. Enormous. Because men will recognize themselves and hate me, their wives will loathe me... The other whores already hate me. Because they say that it does them wrong, that it forces their prices down, it ruins the work. And then what they call the professional secret. Nobody ever made us sign on the dotted line whether or not we had the professional secret, but I mean, it's something occult, more or less. There are women who wish I was dead, because I put the prices in [the book]. They say to themselves, yeah, if this stupid cunt wrote that she sucked off a guy for seventy francs and I always ask for a hundred or a hundred and fifty, well, nobody will give me that anymore. You see. It makes a lot of waves. More or less expected. But serious... So with all this, I'm very conscious that I'm going to make myself hated. But on the other hand, it's the truth. So why hide the truth? Look, if married women could understand how to be nice about sucking their husbands' cocks, putting a finger or two in his ass for love, well, then he wouldn't need to go to whores, all this would be progress for them!

I'm not so sure about that.

Yes it would. Completely. How many clients do I get who say, my wife doesn't want to kiss me on the mouth, she doesn't want to suck my cock, my wife won't touch my asshole, I mean, it's neverending. You listen to these constant litanies... It's true that sexuality with their wives is extremely difficult, impoverished, restrictive, it's boring. Couples' sexuality is BOR-ING.

What if someone said to you, "Listen, I wanna kiss you on the mouth as much as I want."

Yes?

"How much?"

But they do kiss me, you know!

"And you have to get lost in it."

Oh, well look. I say, I'm not in love... I mean, if it's a Turkish immigrant, poor as Job...

... who says that to you, you'd give it to him?

They don't say that to me, poor things! They take me in their arms and kiss me. I let it happen because they need to be...

Just outside on the lips?

Oh! Even a little more, but I fake it. I fake it. I'm not in love with everybody. If I was in love, it would be different.

Do they feel it when you prefer them a little?

I don't prefer anyone.

If it's a gorgeous black man?

Black men in Europe are kings.

Do they come to your place often?

The last one who was here didn't come back again.

When was this?

Oh, not too long ago. Because he saw me in the newspapers. A gorgeous young black. Really handsome.

How old?

Oh! Maybe he was twenty-four. He sat down in my kitchen. He said look, I'm a student, I'm not rich. I said look, that's not my problem. So how about fifty francs? I said no, that doesn't interest me. You should go fuck for free, find yourself a fiancée, a girlfriend, just be nice, a little gallant, it'll work like it's on wheels. I don't have time to waste, go on, go! I kicked him out the door and I never saw him again.

Why didn't you want him?

Because this guy didn't need me.

Even though he was gorgeous?

There was no need for me to fuck around, there wasn't love, he wasn't in love. He said to himself, here's a poor old whore, I'm handsome, I'm black, I'm young, she'll be thrilled to have me on her bed, so I'll offer her the absolute minimum, and then I'll make the most of it. So no way. He left and he didn't get anything.

And who was the last one to have a little love?

They don't have love!

But you wrote hymns to black men in your book![2]

A long time ago, a long time ago. That was in Germany. They were soldiers, they were bored, so they wanted someone to fall in love with them! But here, in Geneva, they're all sons of diplomats, ministers, princes, you understand, and they don't give a fuck at all. They all have good women trotting along after them, so—

There's never been one to come here who you remember in particular?

Yes. There are one or two who are nice. Who are respectful and tender. But there's no real love. You know here, blacks don't pay because all the girls in Geneva want them, they have them up to here. And all the women want to marry them, they want to make babies with them, to get engaged and marriage and everything. It annoys them. So they come to whores to have some peace.

But there aren't any who come from France?

No. It's Arabs who come here from France. Oh, I wouldn't take a black guy for a hundred French francs. Difficult as they are, do you realize!... They're Africans. And Africans aren't famous for their

---

2. *Le Noir est une couleur* (*Black is a Color*).

sensitivity. Because you know that in Africa, women are mutilated, they can't have pleasure. So the men, they're used to fucking hard, you know, and it takes time. It's exhausting, it wears you down, it hurts. There's no tenderness, none at all.

The black guy who came…

That was a black guy from Egypt.

Oh! You like them less. You would have preferred a black guy from North Africa?

Oh! Not at all! They're the worst. I prefer black guys from America. They've suffered; they're much nicer. Africans think they have the right to do anything. They think they're as beautiful as gods, and they are. Knowing this, they're hard, they stay hard, and by the time they ejaculate it's been an hour. You think that's funny?

But you like it!

What? *Quelle horreur*! It kills me. Guys like that!… No way. I prefer black Americans. Because with them, there was love. We really liked each other.

You would have agreed to do the Italian TV show?

I would have found it marvelous to finally tell a real true story.

You know that at one point Véronique cried.

She cried?

Yes. I think it's after the scene with the cop who said to her, "I'm not paying because I'm a cop and I can make trouble for you."

Who did she cry for. For herself?

I don't know.

Over the cop?

She cried.

She cried because she felt trapped.

And the last time that you cried?

(Silence.) Yes, when was it? Oh, yes, I'll tell you, it's because I heard a Ray Charles song, it overwhelmed me. It made me think of the Berber. A song that said, "Give me a last try,"[3] give me one last chance, let me love you, I've failed at everything, it's all my fault.... but let me try one last time. I was moved, I cried listening to this, because I was thinking of the Berber. That was the last time I cried.

---

3. In English in the original.

3

Summer 1981

Jean-Luc Hennig: ...*So Saturday was August 1, the Swiss national holiday. With fanfares, rockets, little flags and paper bombs. The streets are hot tonight, huh? You must have had to keep your shoulder to the wheel!* (Laughter.)

Grisélidis Réal: Well yeah, but Marie-France, who does the fancy neighborhood, she didn't get any work at all Saturday night. She called me, it was two thirty in the morning. I had just gotten into bed to sleep, she said, I didn't get any work, not one single client! Well, I did seventeen!

Seventeen on Saturday!

Yeah, immigrant laborers who don't give much of a shit for the Swiss patriotic holiday. Well, they came to fuck at my place, it was much better.

Spanish guys?

Turks, Arabs, Spanish, Portuguese, more or less tipsy but adorable, adorable. You should have, it's too bad, you should have hidden somewhere! The seventeenth, I couldn't go on anymore, and there was still one outside the door and one down in the street, I said no,

I can't do it anymore. They could see in my eyes it wasn't possible. At a certain point, my vagina kind of started hurting.

Really?

Oh yes. It practically breaks the skin by the end. No, but I realized something extraordinary. By the seventeenth, I had absolutely no strength left, and then I said to myself, well, fundamentally, where am I? Am I still myself? Or have I stopped existing? Do I exist differently? And then I saw that something kind of marvelous had happened to me, you can collectivize your body.

What?

Yes. I mean, you stay yourself, but at the same time, you belong to others, I was myself all the bodies of the other people who'd come here. I wasn't only their body, but their penis, their soul, their race, I became totally multiple. It's wonderful. You're like a piece of algae tangled up in other algae. It's an ocean. All the nuances are mixed together. It's absolute splendor.

But it's been happening to you for years.

Yes, sure! But Saturdays like this, it's only happened to me twice to do seventeen. One time last October, and then this past Saturday. You shouldn't think that it's always like this. I mean, I wouldn't hold out, and you can see perfectly well that I live almost like a poor person.

Seventeen, how long does that take?

Oh! All day and all night! Because I don't rush them, but…

It started at 3 in the afternoon?

Yes, right, 3 in the afternoon. And then I ran out to do a few errands, but very quickly.

It didn't stop?

No, it was exhausting, killing, but killing and marvelous. I mean, by the seventeenth you're completely drugged. You're in this state, a human being crushed under a steamroller. You're totally drained. How can I explain it? You're totally emptied of all aggression. You know, to give birth without pain, they teach you how to breathe, they tell you, you're like a rag, look, they lift your arm and it drops... Well! You're in the same state, you have no reflexes left, no more resources, and that's how it works the best.

Then he could have killed you, the seventeenth?

Well look. I made another fantastic discovery, the sweeter you are, the more spineless you are, without nerves, without reactions, the better it goes. Because fundamentally what they want isn't to hurt you, or to kill you, or bore you, what they want is for you to be nice, that's all. So since you're totally amorphous, practically emptied of your substance, emptied of all your strength, of what gets on your nerves, well, you're so malleable, so sweet, so agreeable that that's how it goes the best. There weren't any snags. Because when I get annoyed the men get annoyed too. We end up coming to insults and even to blows, and that's just the beginning. You see, the man tenses up, and after that it goes much worse. But when you're sweet, humane, superhumanly sweet, well, they're so sweet and happy, confident... That's it, total confidence, so it's very important to have discovered this.

So you didn't do anything on Sunday?

Nine! Look, do you wanna see the laundry? Because I bathed at the sink to keep things going fast enough. The panties are still in the laundry, there are nine, you can count 'em.

You must be completely exhausted.

Not at all. I'm in great shape. Because I slept. I sleep without sleeping pills, without anything. I drank two orange juices, look, we'll have a cup of coffee, I feel great. But you don't realize, it recharges your batteries. Even though after the last one, last night, I thought he wouldn't come, I went ouf! But I spent the whole evening putting my paperwork in order, you can take a look, it's fabulous. And then a poor guy showed up at two in the morning! So at that point, unfortunately, I'd kind of recharged my nerves, so I started yelling, I said, no way. At two in the morning! You always show up at the last minute!

Who was this guy?

Oh, it's the one who's always wasted, who fell into a coma on my carpet! He gets attached, he comes back, he keeps coming back, I have to take him.... So I said, "Naturally you've had too much to drink as usual, and it's two in the morning!" And his head fell. He's a short little guy, when he's drunk he speaks Italian, but otherwise he speaks Spanish. *(Laughter.)* I swear! So he said, but I'm just getting off work, I couldn't come earlier. When I asked him if he'd had too much to drink, he made a little sign to say yes, well not that much, not that much... He couldn't deny it, he smelled like alcohol. Then I looked him up and down and I said, you'd better be nice, meaning this better not drag on for three hours, and you better not collapse and faint like last time. But he promised me that he'd be nice, that he'd be careful. Well, he was adorable. He even gave me an extra ten francs. The more you yell the nicer they are. I'm telling you though, in the end, it's better to be a little rag, all sweet, that's how you have the best human interactions. Nobody wants to hurt you. Quite the opposite, they're overjoyed to have you be nice like that. Look, you have to be available, and you have to be very tired above all. You can't be doped up. It's the fatigue itself that becomes a kind of luminosity. As though you're radiating light, it's fantastic, you're like a jellyfish in the water. *(Laughter.)* You know, the speeches they read at Barbès, eighty Arabs over the weekend, I said to myself, these poor women must be more than wrecks, they're totally dehumanized, they must be half dead. I saw it as enormous suffering, they were crushed. Well, now I'm sure that it's the opposite. Obviously there's a moment of total emptiness, but that emptiness does you good, it's fantastic! Instead of being here, always worrying about what's going wrong in your little brain, well by the end there's no more brain, everything goes great. It's like surfing. You float, it's like some kind of immobile ecstasy. No effort, no problems. It's a divine state, frankly. Maybe that's divinity. Completely letting yourself go…

But you've never felt that before?

Not to that degree. Because before, I fought against that state of non-being. I struggled to maintain myself, like a plant fighting to stay upright in a storm. But this time there was a moment where I didn't have the strength anymore. I'd felt that a tiny bit during my second grape cure, because I got to the twentieth day and then too, I'd almost dematerialized, and in the end I found that the bodies of men had become so beautiful, the flesh had become so attractive, so agreeable to look at and to touch, and that doesn't happen in this profession very often, quite the opposite, you always see the defects, bad smells... And in summer they reek! There's even one, it's the first time I've heard of something like this, one who apologized for it, with an accent, I don't know if he was Spanish or what! I swear, you bathe in something like an animal stink, of sweat, it's the great sweat of summer. The great sweat of love. You try to ignore it, it reeks, and in reality it's extraordinary, like music. *(Laughter.)*

This state of total abandon, did they feel it or not?

Them, they lived it, we lived it together, you see. And then they were all super excited. We had to be careful not to let it go too fast. I'm the one who's always telling you the men don't get hard enough, well here, we had to be very careful, they were ejaculating at high speed. The fireworks weren't on the harbor, they were right here on my bed. Ah! It's a pleasure to tell you, believe me, we had to be careful, because they were squirting all over the place, in five seconds we were done!

You told me the other day, there was one who showed up, saw the unmade bed, and plunged right into it.

Well yeah, that was Albert. I couldn't stop him. He was already naked and lying in the bed as though it were his. I couldn't say "Albert, get up, let me make the bed, I'll put the work sheets on." I couldn't, he took me by surprise.

So you got in bed?

I had to! In my bed. It was the same sheets that were here.

The little sheets with flowers.

… Little red flowers.

That never happens?

Never. Come on! All the whores will tell you. We don't fuck inside the bed. Once I saw an adorable old whore in Lyon, I mean her, I think she didn't give a shit and maybe she even liked it. She opened a drawer to show me, and she said voilà, here are my piles of sheets, and the bed was totally open. I found it very mysterious and unusual. Because it's not done.

You wouldn't like sleeping in a bed where men had come?

No! Look, you know, some of them beg to spend the night with me! They'd give me a thousand Swiss francs, I say no!

Why?

At least I have the right to sleep in peace by myself at night. No way! It would be impossible!

But you've done it?

Oh! Once or twice for some young man I'd more or less fallen in love with. I got over that fast, because I saw it was worthless. No, you know that Friday night somebody got really mad at me because basically, I met a tall young man, with a beard, so drunk he couldn't stand up. He explained that he'd been at a friend's birthday party. He couldn't even talk, he couldn't walk, I practically had to carry him here, but what can I say, I needed money. And overall he seemed nice, and I said to myself, I'll manage to get him hard and make him come, for sure. He'd given me a hundred francs, and that's very decent for me, to get a hundred Swiss francs, that can be hard to get. The poor guy, though, it was long, long long…

Was he Swiss?

Yes. Dark curly hair. Gorgeous boy. I mean, I realized I wasn't getting it. In the end he told me the truth, that he didn't live alone. He lived in a city, much further away, with a lesbian girl-friend. So I concluded, logically, that this girlfriend, since she likes girls, she probably didn't put too much effort in with him, so he was frustrated, there was something that just didn't work between them. People don't just come to us, you know, unless there's a serious problem. So this young man, he just wouldn't come, he wouldn't come. I'd deployed every resource of my imagination, my technique. In the end he got there, I mean, it was a miracle. And the poor thing, he just fell asleep on my bed he was so drunk. I said no, no. Get up! You can't sleep here! It was three in the morning, you know? I couldn't wake him. So I got him up by force, and he begged me, he said, you know, I'm in pain right now, just let me sleep here, I can't get up now, I'm so exhausted, exhausted, exhausted! And I won't be able to drive my car. That was true; it was worrying. So in the end I gave him a glass of mineral water. He offered to empty his bank account for me, I mean, he would have done anything to sleep here, he said, I'll even sleep on the carpet, I said, that's out of the question! I mean, in this kind of situation you feel really cruel. I said no. And I kicked him out of here, severely, and he might have died in a car accident. But I don't want to get ground down to the wire. I can't take that. They don't realize!

And the two young guys who followed you the other night, why didn't you take them?

Because there had been a huge newspaper headline "Spectacular Escape at Bochuz." Bochuz is the prison. So when there are spectacular escapes, you can expect that these escaped convicts are going to show up around here, in the whore neighborhood, and obviously, they're going to find themselves a victim, they probably have no choice. In the first place because they need to hide somewhere at night, and to steal money, because they're broke, and it's just dangerous. After escapes, it's always dangerous. You really have to be careful. And me, when I saw one young guy and then another, following me obstinately, I flat out refused them. I don't take risks like that. I mean, there are always problems with the young ones. Really, because they're either on drugs or they've drunk too much, or they're guys who are just in the shit, aggressive, and they have no money and ill will. They can go as far as murdering you, raping you, robbing you!

You've never had an escaped convict?

Oh! Years ago, I refused a guy in a red shirt, he'd escaped from a psychiatric asylum in Basel. I found out the following day from a girl. I had the intuition to refuse him, but he kept insisting. He even took out a hundred franc note. But I had the intuition, I don't know why, to refuse him, he had a bizarre look about him. Well, that guy was armed and he'd escaped from an asylum. But there are plenty of guys like that running around, it's normal.

Where do you stand at night?

I walk, I take these little trips, my own trajectories around the neighborhood, there's what I call the "grand tour" and then the "petit tour."

What's the "grand tour"?

That's when there are no clients, so I have to do something. I do this whole street, I go down, I take the rue de Berne, first I do the "petit tour," and when I see it's not working, I cross, I go stand in front of the bookstore, I look at the books to encourage myself, I look to see if there are taxi lines, when there are taxi lines you know that there's no work. If the taxis aren't working, we don't either. So then, I have to go as far as the train station, go back down, go back up, it's exhausting!

You don't like going out as much, lately?

What? I love it. I have marvelous outfits for the night. I have a fox fur, with paws, I have two of them. One of them has the head and paws, they're gorgeous! You have no idea how much I love it. And then to go have a drink at the bar, listen to some accordion, I mean, it's divine! You know, it's a little life à la Francis Carco, you walk up and down the sidewalk in your clicking heels. You have to be careful not to twist your ankle, it's happened to me before, you have no idea, it's an adventure!

Are there a lot of girls walking around at night, or do they just stand somewhere, ready and waiting?

I might be the only one who really walks. I love walking. I love moving, and it's less boring than just standing there, and people don't realize as much that you're a whore if you walk. But there are other girls who just stand there courageously, practically, at the door of their hotel or building. And when they get sick of standing there, they just go to the bar next door or across the street.

But they never go very far, I've noticed.

No, they never go very far. It's like their turf, you know. Animals have their turf, you know, Indians too, they have places. Look, it's your territory, your turf, your little spot, where you park your feet. It reassures them in a way. If you take them two houses further on, they feel a little worried... They feel a little uprooted. Have you noticed that? But I feel like the night belongs to me. The night is beautiful.

Dressed all in black?

Oh! No, sometimes all in red or all in white, it depends. I have a lot of work outfits that you haven't seen.

Really?

Sure. I have fabulous things, I have a pair of fur shorts that I've only worn once, trembling, because I said to myself, it's probably a little ridiculous at my age. The guys were following me, you should have seen it!

Panther shorts? Lynx?

Like Tarzan's wife, a tiny little fur, so you have to wear high stockings, black or gold, and then a little shirt, low-cut, and then I guarantee you there's a... a terrible allure! There are herds of men following you. They move like one single man and they pursue you. It's like a hunt. You become an animal, with a pack of hounds behind you hunting you down. Look, I'm going to drink out of the little cup the Berber made for me in prison. But he put it on a little hotplate and it's kind of burnt. He made it himself, for me. Nice, huh?...

And in the daytime?

Yeah, well, that's why I'm sick of living in this neighborhood. Because you're here full time. You go out and there are three Spanish guys that detatch themselves from some wall and start following you, they have no concept of why or how it might not be your working hours. They just don't understand. It's awful! So you walk down the street, but you're never at ease. You hear ksst ksst, or woo-hoo. Oh! I mean, sometimes, I'm outside myself. I turn around and I say, come on, I'm not a dog! But they don't understand French. I mean, you know, it frays your nerves!

They look at you when you walk down the street?

Yeah, well, they turn around.

And other women?

Listen, there's a whole group of women who smile at me, we stop... Yesterday night, I saw a few, we kiss each other on the cheek, ask each other how it's going, we tell our little stories, it's wonderful. Some of them hate me, but I have no idea why. So too bad. You just gotta walk straight... There are looks of hate, whistles, even insults, often. But who knows why. So it's lucky I'm not in a whore building. Because you know, watch in hand, they watch every little thing you do. They spy on everything, everything. You bring a client up, they want to know how much time you stayed with him, what you did, how much he paid. They know everything. They keep tabs, and then it's insults, fights, endless catfights. "You stayed five minutes too long!... And you're lowering the prices... And that's my client, not yours!..." It's horrific. Fight after fight! The other day, a wonderful woman came here, to my place. I mean, she gets insulted constantly, they treat her like an old hag! But these little cunts, one day they'll be old too. They don't think about that. And then being young doesn't mean they know any better how to live. Not at all. On the contrary. When I saw this admirable woman who is sixty-five years old, the dignity she has, the calm… She's lived her whole life on the sidewalk. She's raised two kids, she doesn't have a cent saved up. I mean, a tiny sum, not even worth talking about. I mean, I find this beautiful. A woman who has totally given herself. When you see women like this, you realize that these little parakeets, they haven't understood anything, haven't lived anything, they have plenty of time to get their faces broken and start drooling. A woman like this is a monument! She had her little dog. A little poodle, white as snow.

Do a lot of girls have dogs?

Yes. I tried to get one a few times, but… You have to take them out to pee in the morning, I had to get up too early. I have too many things to do. The revolution takes up all my time, I don't have time for dogs. One time I had little cats, because I was depressed, but let me tell you that my depression ended the day they were gone, I mean, that's what cured me for good. They were marvelous, but they ran all over the place. Clients would come in and they'd jump on top of them. There was one guy who'd barely put his boxers down and the three cats were already on top of them. I went toward the bidet and there were two cats in it. Come on! It just wasn't possible anymore. Little Siamese. Siamese crossed with tiger cats. They were like a horde. I couldn't put a piece of laundry down, or a bra, or a bank receipt, nothing. They were always on top of every-thing, playing with it, getting it dirty with their paws, dragging it through the dust… And when I wanted to do a client, all three of them would be on top of him licking him all over, running under his arms, on his shoulders, in his hair…

They scratch a little, don't they?

Yeah, that too. So the men were scared, you understand, of getting scratch marks from the cats, cause then their wives would think they'd gone to a sadistic hooker! *(Laughter.)*

So Fat Robert died in the spring?

Yes. Apparently there were a thousand people at his funeral. It was covered in flowers. I couldn't go; I had an appointment at the Palais des Nations with the president of the journalists. I was in a rage, by the way. I wanted to be at that funeral.

But you had gone to see him at the chapel.

La Chapelle des Rois. Yes. I brought a rose that I'd had here in a vase. I went with my friend Richard, and they didn't want to let us see him. Apparently even the family didn't see him. You know that Fat Robert was enormous, and well, apparently he had swollen to twice his size. Yes. Because of the gasses. They might have had to cut him into pieces to fit him in the coffin; even the family didn't see him. There was a door, it was a refrigerator, at so many degrees below zero, with a tiny little window, and well, the old guard didn't even want to turn the light on so we could see his head, nothing.

Is it true that the window of his café, at the time, still had "The fat guy is still in the furnace" written on it?

It's still written on it. We can go see it anytime. It's next door, Fat Robert's bar. And now, there's a little sign with a cross drawn in ink, that says "Closed due to decease." It's a very sad story.

He died in May?

Yes. And you know, when *Le Fou Parle*[1] came out, I was panicked because I said to myself… to have written the clients' names… That really harmed some people; they are really indignant and miserable… So Fat Robert, I don't know how he got his hands on *Le Fou parle*, I only found out about it from a woman a long time afterward; apparently he was livid. But I doubted it. I'll explain it to you, the same night that *Le Fou parle* was circulating around the neighborhood, because there were at least six ladies who were pissed, who found the whole thing so funny, they passed it around in the bar, I mean, this *Fou parle* could be seen from afar, it had a black cover, you know, it went all over the neighborhood. Like a trail of powder! So me, I said, my god, Robert, he's gonna see this. So I got the fuck out of the bar. I was a bit cowardly, I kissed him on the cheek and I said to myself, this is really a Judas kiss, but I have to get out of here, I can't stay here any longer, I can't breathe, I didn't expect *Le Fou parle* to get all around the bar and end up in the hands of Fat Robert. But I think that's what happened. And the next day, Fat Robert, without calling, showed up here, he knocked at my door, I opened and there he was in front of me, you know, like an angry elephant, and he looked at me steadily, without talking, and there was immense suffering in his gaze, and terrible anger. I mean, he was famous for his tantrums. I stayed there without moving. I looked at him and I poured into my gaze all the peace and humility I could. Asking his forgiveness without saying anything. Well, he didn't say anything either. He came in, he made love as usual, he drank some whiskey, I put on some music for him, he gave me a hundred francs, and voilà. We never spoke about it. I mean, maybe he'd come to throw a tantrum, who knows. He didn't say anything. You see, the dignity of this man.

---

1. The journal in which *The Little Black Book* was first published.

Do you generally learn about the death of your clients?

No. Usually we don't even know who they really are. But he didn't hide from anyone that he was a client. He used to say it in public, even. He told me once that in a café, there was a woman, kind of dark-skinned, lovely, and very young. He greeted her, like "Hi, what's up, how's it going? You mean you don't recognize your old clients anymore?" Apparently she'd made a few gestures to keep from having to say anything. So he said, "Come on, are you ashamed of me or something?" I mean look, this is the opposite of what usually happens. Usually, you see the clients walking right by with a fixed gaze, you absolutely mustn't recognize them, not even wink at them, nothing. As though there were something to be ashamed of. As though it would be some kind of humiliation. *(Silence.)* There are dead people I love more than the living. I mean, I have a whole family of the dead, girlfriends who committed suicide, great artists who couldn't bear life any longer... Poets dead of heart attacks... For me they're people who still exist. They live with me, we talk to each other, we have a lot to say to each other. Like Fat Robert, he's come to me I don't know how many times since he died. I know very clearly when he's here. We talk. I mean, he takes up so much space when he comes that I can barely breathe, he sucks all the oxygen out of the room. When he was dead in his fridge and the super didn't want to show him to me, I understood very well that he [Fat Robert] hadn't wanted people to see him. Toward the end, he'd talk to you through the door, he'd say, Leave me alone, it's not your problem, I'm not really myself right now, the way I am now, if you please have the kindness to leave me in peace. So we'd leave. And anyway, a refriger-ated man who might have been cut into pieces, it would have really caused him grief to know that people would have come to look at him. On the other hand he was glad we'd come, this I know. He was touched. Even the rose, that the super said to throw in the trash, I know that Robert must have known I'd brought him a rose. They know everything, the dead, don't you think?

Did you have a little crush on him?

Oh it's unfortunate, I just don't have the time! I don't have the time. And you know, love, it's so delicate and complicated, I mean, I've aged, unfortunately. So it doesn't go the way it used to, at thirty or even at forty. I'll be fifty-two. Who am I supposed to find to have a crush on? I could get myself twelve little Arabs without papers or money or a place to live. I could bring them all back here. They'll adore me! But then you end up with the worst hassle, because what they want is your cash, I mean, your ass, they don't give a fuck, because they get that everywhere. But if they can get that from you too, they'll take it. Aside from that they just become your dependents. And they get mean.

But there isn't a little love affair among your clients? One who comes, you know, a little too often... a little too easily?

... Oh! I guess there's a doctor, he's adorable. But the poor guy, the last time he came here I was in the middle of making photocopies, right here, I was half crazy, I had to send out a ton of documents to Paris, and I wouldn't even let him in I was a little hard with him, I said, No, you have to call first, it's not gonna work right now. And he was so disappointed.

Did he come from far away?

No. He probably lives in Geneva. I mean, look, there are clients I like, but they're always the ones who are a little strange. Like the one I wrote into the little book, you know, the musician who's a little like some *pierrot lunaire*... He's extraordinary, that one.

You like him?

Yes, I like him. A lot. He's very pale, very magnetic and mysterious, it takes a very long time to make him come, but it's never a question. Love isn't only sex, I think it's spiritual more than anything else.

Really?

Love is magnetic, spiritual more than everything else. I mean, I'm reading a book right now that's fascinating. Have you read *Le Monde éternel des éons*?[2]

Is love a question of eons?

Certainly. I think love is something invisible, untouchable, undefinable, it's spiritual magnetism, you know? It's like electricity. You don't see it coming or going, something surges through you and ignites you, leaves you breathless or completely spellbound, and then you can't really withhold or possess, it's really something extraordinary, it's completely mysterious.

How did you see your Berber...

Well at first we understood each other through the eyes, because when I saw him for the first time it was in the prison visiting room, in front of five cops. It was extraordinary, and afterward we held hands. We couldn't really talk because the cops were listening, so you don't have your own words, you're forced to hide everything. Most things have to pass between you in silence. What you say in front of cops is meaningless. It's bullshit. It's for the

---

2. *The Eternal World of Eons.*

cops. But what you say with your eyes, with your hands, what the cops can neither hear nor understand, this real language, it happens there, in a prison visiting room. All prisoners and their wives understand this.

You told me that Arabs are kind of touching because they make love in a kind of homey way, they take you in their arms, they have a tendency to treat you like a wife...

What I meant was... Moroccans are very affectionate. They love a woman's body, they want to explore it, to touch it, breathe it in, embrace it, I mean, they'll cover you in kisses, which of course means you're drenched in saliva. Whereas other Arabs are a little rougher. I mean, some of them will stab you. They put their hands on your head like this, I mean, a little harder and they could break your neck. *(Laughter.)* Portuguese guys, with them it's the opposite, they take you by the shoulders and they go hhiin.... So your head's about to knock against the wall. I thought I'd crack my head open more than once. I'd put my hands behind my head, but I was afraid I'd end up with broken fingers! It's unbelievable, the brutality... But it's an amorous brutality. It's not malevolent brutality.

Do they smother you sometimes?

Oh, well there's one I call "Three Tons." A Spanish guy, yeah! He smothers you, he crushes you, you can't breathe. You don't know where to put your head, your mouth, your eyes or your nose, because you're just gonna choke. It's scary. But what do you want? It's love... *(Laughter.)*

You still have to tell me that magnificent story about the boy who was in love with a transvestite.

The tall blond prince… Oh yeah, he was really handsome. I'm not often attracted to men who aren't exotic or Middle-Eastern. I mean, Swiss men are a little drab. It's a mean thing to say, but what do you want, it's true. I don't think people are usually strongly attracted to their own race. Contrasts are a lot more affecting, much more mysterious. So this young blond guy, he was completely nordic, I think he was Swiss, and normally, nothing about him would have attracted me. But he had such a candid, luminous air about him, he was tall, beautiful, with cerulean blue eyes, beautiful blond hair, sunny, and very white skin. You could have taken him for a dancer. But, with this candid way about him, I said to myself, he's gonna be a lot of work. Or else he's a little shithead who just got out of the can with his angelface, and he's gonna K.O. me, steal everything I own, and rape me on top of everything else. You're always on your guard, you know, because anything could happen to you, any minute of the day. I know a woman who had nothing happen to her in twenty-six years in the business, and in the end some guy who went up to her studio with her, and he took out a pistol and pointed it at her, she had to run away naked, she's over fifty, running down the hallway screaming. Do you see what I mean? In a way it's what can make for the charm of this kind of life. You're always at the mercy of the unexpected.

So, the cerulean?

Alright. I was eating in a little bar where you can't eat anymore, they don't serve food there anymore. And he was looking at me, yeah. He was looking at me the whole time. I may be myopic, but I could see what was happening. Eventually he sat down next to me and he ordered some food too. And he was still looking at me. So, one thing led to another, and he started talking to me.

Was he very young?

He was nineteen. This is what was really worrying. The younger a boy is, the surer you are that he has no money. And if he has a sexual problem, if he's totally repressed, he could be mean. And if he doesn't have any cash, it's like the other one who wanted to rape me, they absolutely want what they want, but they can't pay. And on top of that they want to get revenge on their mothers. Or their grandmothers. All this makes for powerful aggression. They're made of dynamite, these young ones. It's nothing like the old tired daddies, I mean, at least with them, you know they're not going to murder you. So alright, he was eating, and then he said to me, You work in the neighborhood? I hesitated a little, just to avoid taking too many risks. I said yes, yeah, well it depends. *(Laughter.)* He was a little worried, he must have said to himself, maybe I've made a mistake. He was a little embarrassed, but after he saw that he hadn't mistaken me for a whore. So he asked me if he could accompany me home. I said sure, but why? Oh! You know, just because! I think you're nice. I'd like to talk with you a little. Well, ok, talking's fine, he's not gonna murder me in the street. Although anything can happen in all these little dark corners, there are women who've had their bags stolen, they got punched in the face, people found them unconscious on the ground, bathed in their own blood. You've got to be really careful in this neighborhood. Alright, so we were walking, walking, and then he said, I would like very much to accompany you home. I said, sure, but do you have any money? Yes, yes, of course. I just got my paycheck. I said, yeah, but it's much too expensive for you. I wanted to discourage him completely. He said no, no. I'd be glad to give you a hundred francs. So I said oh yeah, show me! *(Laughter.)* And in the end, he was very nice, not timid, kind, well-spoken. I brought him here, but I was still very worried, I mean, it really isn't normal, a tall handsome boy, nineteen years old, not crippled, I mean, what did he want? Why would he come here? I am much older than he is. At this point in his life he should go to a beautiful young whore! Some of them are eighteen years old. As beautiful as day. I mean, that's more exciting for a young man than to be with an old mother. Look, it's a little perverse. It created a kind of anguish. Given the age difference. And given the inexplicable attraction they have for older women. So this young man was here, naked, very beautiful. He'd given me a hundred francs, so I was starting to feel kind of reassured. I'd washed him, dried him, and he was almost hard already. I said to myself, this is even more worrisome, since he apparently doesn't have some kind of problem. So what's gonna happen? What's he gonna do? My God, what will happen? Well, you can't show that you're afraid. Because you're already in an inferior state. You're already half murdered if you show that you're afraid. I stayed totally at ease, very maternal, and he stretched out on the bed, I sucked him the usual way, his hard-on was perfectly good. He had a gorgeous cock, long, very muscular, very firm. Young and beautiful. I said, but he doesn't have a single problem? Then what the fuck is he doing here? But I figured it out after a little while. Because he was hard, sure, he was hard for this, but there wasn't anything else. I'm telling you, I tried everything. You have to suck everywhere. So, ok, he was still hard, but he never ejaculated. I said to him, have you ever made love to a woman? And there he said, yes, no. It was a little bizarre, he said no, it wasn't really a woman, it was a transvestite. She's a dancer. And I'm really in love. I love her. I said, that's great! You should stay with her! Yes, but I still wanted to see if I could also make love to a real woman. So I said, you really shouldn't worry about it. We'll try. It should go fine. That's when I tried doggy style, to give him some confidence, because guys, between each other, when they assfuck each other, they're more used to seeing each other from the back, it's less feminine. Because women's butts aren't as muscular and firm. It's nothing like a man's ass. Except for very young women who have admirable little posteriors, but at my age, it's not really the same thing. Especially not after four kids. I did my maximum. I swear to you, I was at pains! I tried everything. Nothing worked. And he was still hard, despite everything. It was at this point that a crisis can start, when the guy realizes he can't come, some of them don't think. They'll strangle a woman or kill her just to finally ejaculate. Most sexual murders are probably this kind of thing. Just to finally empty their balls. There's such nervous tension, it must be awful for guys. They must just not know how to get to the end, and at that point they kill.

And this one, what did he do?

I didn't want him to be sad. Because he was too handsome and too kind. I said, look, it's not a big deal. Go back to your transvestite friend, make love with her, that'll be more beautiful and much better for you, I'm sure. And then one day maybe, if you fall in love with a young woman, well, give it a try. Because, deep down, you really don't have a problem. We just didn't click. But you could click very quickly with someone, one day. I just think it would be better if you were in love.

Did he pay?

I wouldn't have done a thing if he hadn't paid. No, come on, what do you expect! I'm not the Salvation Army over here.

And then he left?

Unfortunately, yes. Sometimes you encourage them, tell them to masturbate, there are formulas for this, you say to them, Oh! It would be so great if you would touch yourself and I'll do the same thing. You fake it, of course.

And he didn't do it?

No! No, no. He didn't ejaculate. Poor young man! But that wasn't my fault. I mean, I can't be a transvestite! *(Laughter.)*

(Silence.)... You know, the Berber, I'm the one who taught him everything. Since he had always made love with boys, since he was a professional gigolo. Aside from that he had lovers. Young, younger than he was. He'd also had some women, but always prostitutes in Paris, a little woman who was on drugs all the time, and another who liked women. But you see, he'd never really had a truly normal love relationship with a woman. He did it like a Tunisian hussar. I mean, these guys treat us like animals; I wouldn't be surprised if they have sex with goats and donkeys. They lift your legs up to the ceiling, and rrrran! How do you wanna give pleasure to a woman like that, it's impossible. It's monstrous! I said, that's not the way to make love. I explained a few things to him. He became an excellent student. In fact he told me, I will be grateful to you all my life to have taught me how to make a woman come, with every possible detail, every imaginable nuance. He got a taste for it, he became an artist. Nice, huh? So now he knows how to make boys *and* girls come. He has two strings in his bow. *(Laughter.)*

But I didn't know that it was because of him that you went back to...

To streetwalking.

How did it happen?

When I had a little bit of money set aside, well, the Berber got out of prison. He didn't have anything...

So it was for love?

I do everything for love. You know that. Even this book I'm doing with you, in a certain sense... So, when he got out of prison, I had to take charge of him completely. I had to go pick him up in Tunis, pay for a new passport for him, we had to go to a police station every day, it was exhausting. The atmosphere was terrifying. Afterwards, we managed to leave Tunisia by plane, and we landed in Italy. He met up with some old friends. Old tricks of his, really sweet. Eventually we came to Paris, because he's forbidden entry into Switzerland. Now, though, he's been kicked out everywhere. So what do you expect, we got to Paris, and there, for five months, day and night we looked for a job for him and we couldn't find one. In the end he became such an alcoholic, so violent that we broke up, because it wasn't working at all between us, and I'd started participating in these political struggles for women prostitutes, with the last money I had, I was living on fifteen hundred francs a month by the end... I said to myself I have to start making a living again. And since I was part of this prostitutes' struggle that fascinated me, I said to myself, I should go back to the sidewalk and try to demystify, totally, what goes on there. And more than that, the sidewalk gives you a lot of freedom, because your schedule is up to you, you don't have a boss. It's important to say that in Switzerland we are free whores. Totally free. You get up when you want to. You hit the pavement when you feel like it, and if you want to live on a strict daily minimum, you can manage it, if you want to save up some money and work the pavement full time, you do it, if you're healthy enough, if you've got the will. I mean, you do exactly as you please. It might be the only profession in the world in which you are totally free. Of every constraint, of every obligation. People don't realize this. Even now, at the UN, prostitution is considered as a kind of slavery. I can tell you that it's the opposite. Except that look, you absolutely have to be in a country where the laws aren't against you. In Switzerland, we're considered to be citizens who live an improper life, but aside from that, you're free to make a living, you pay your taxes, you pay your rent, you have peace.

Have you read Roselyne's book, La Maculée*?[3] [The Blood-Stained Woman]. She's a sadomasochist on the rue Saint-Denis, and she tells some pretty horrible things; I've paid attention to these things. There are clients who show up with a suitcase full of stinging nettles, and they want all the thorns on their body. There's one who comes with two birds in each hand, and squeak squeak, until he's strangled them!*

That's awful…

There's another who comes with a red iron, he wants to be tattooed [sic] on the chest; another, she has to put needles into his stomach, and there's one who brings a billy club with lead at the end, and she has to beat him until he can't move…

That's crazy.

And another one, she has to cut up his balls with a razor blade.

That's too much!

And she has to sew it all up with string. There's one, she does his nipples with escargot tongs.

Oh, well, we use clothespins and things like that all the time, it's very common.

---

3. Atwood, Jane. *La Maculée*, Ramsay, 1981.

She also talks about "soupeurs," they come from behind and lick another guy's come.

Yes, people do that a lot. I refuse to do stuff like that.

And then some of them, she has to spit in their faces...

Oh, well that's common.

Or she has to burn them with cigarettes, on their backs, or brush them like dogs...

Yes, yes.

There's another one too, he had strips of skin cut from his chest.

That's insane!

And then the ones who eat piss or things like that.

Yes, that's very common too.

You, I think you kind of tell them stories these days?

Right now I try to exhaust myself as little as possible, because you can do everything with words, you know, fantasy has to do with the imagination, and it's much wiser just to tell stories. You see, when you have a masochist lying on your bed, you say to him, "Oh! You know, I'm gonna lock you in a cage and you'll be on all fours in front of a trough of piss, and a trough of shit, and you'll be handcuffed in a dog collar, and I'm gonna beat you through the bars, I'll make you eat the shit and drink the piss, and you'll stay in there for two hours." Then you see, the time it takes to imagine all that, the work is done, they get a little hard, and you finish them off in front of the sink or wherever. It's much simpler. I describe scenes of fantastic torture!

For example?

I have this one bearded guy who is completely nuts. I mean, I don't always have the strength to take him, so I sent him to Chantal or Odette, but sometimes he comes here anyway. After a while you can't get rid of them.

How old is he?

Let's see, him... He must be around sixty. He still lives with his mommy, they're always stuck to their mommy. These mommies are criminals, cunts, I'd like to skin them!

So him, what does he want?

With him, I tell him that I'm gonna eat him alive, on low heat, I'm gonna peel big strips of skin off him, I lick the blood, I piss in his wounds, I mean I don't do it, but I do it in words. And he's in heaven, listening to all this. Now and then he lets out a little chortle, he really experiences it in himself. And right at the end, when he's managed to ejaculate, thanks to imaginary tortures, he says to me, "You're really gonna do all that to me!" I say, of course! Meaning, yeah, I'll do all that to you, but worse! "Oh! So you love me?" "Of course I love you, I'll watch you die!" "Oh! Oh, Solange, oh, this's amazing!" So they're in ecstasy!

Do you ever get really huge guys? Gruesome giants?

Oh, I carried one out of here the other day, and Italian, totally wasted. A glass armoire. He started bickering, opening his fly, I said whoa! Don't bother, and I opened the door the way I always do, and I said, "This isn't going to work. You have to leave." So him, he didn't wanna leave, he continued to open his fly, he didn't wanna pay, he wanted to lower the price, and on top of that he could barely stand up, he was drunk, I mean, he was a brute, so I punched him and I pushed him outside with all my strength, and by the time he realized what had happened to him he was on the other side of the door, but it wasn't easy. You can't let too much time pass, you have to evacuate them from the room in a quarter second, otherwise they could break your face, or worse.

It must have made an awful racket.

Oh, I scream at them, you know, and have panic attacks, I insult them...

The building must be on fire and soaked in blood all the time.

Not at all. The other night, the upstairs neighbors were partying until two in the morning. There was jazz, music blaring, the sound of bottles, I said so much the better, everyone makes his own noise. No no. These are like old folkloric shanties, totally bohemian. Downstairs, the Portuguese, they almost murdered a woman. Even I had to go bang on their door with my fists. Because I was afraid they were killing this poor Portuguese woman, she was howling, howling in Portuguese. There were two guys with evil faces who opened the door. I said "What's going on here?—Oh, she's sick, she's sick.—Well aren't you ashamed to beat up a woman like that, you'd better stop!" I was brave, I could have gotten myself killed. After that they stopped hitting her. It was a domestic scene. Or else they were all high, I don't know, or drunk. But there was shrieking at four in the afternoon, it was horrendous. You shouldn't think that I'm the only one. The whole neighborhood is full of fistfights, there have even been murders. There's been everything. You don't realize. I pass practically unnoticed in all this.

And the girls who show up in the neighborhood for the first time? The brand-new ones?

Oh, not longer ago than two nights ago, I went to eat in a little restaurant, where I have one or two girlfriends I like a lot, and we were talking with a friend who was about to leave for vacation, and she said, there's no more work, there's no more work. I said yes, it's because of the massage parlors and the recession, and she said it's not just that, with all these pieces of news coming in nonstop, this place is full of young girls working the street!

Very very young girls?

Oh yes, eighteen, nineteen years old. Sometimes they're even seventeen. And apparently there are even younger ones!

But when they show up like that, aren't they kind of powerless, a little thrown, they don't really know how to...

Oh, the young girls around now are very clever, a lot more clever than I was at their age, they already understand everything, they simply do what the others do. It's very easy, on one hand. You see, all the old social workers will tell you it's the opposite, that they're plunged into hell, that these poor little darlings sob night and day begging to be saved, but that's not true at all. They are very pleased with themselves. They're beautiful, they're young, they enjoy insane success, you just have to put yourself in their place. Little girls who've been dragged through the shit all through their youth, some of them have been in prison, or reform school, orphanages, they've never had any pleasure in their lives, and they show up here, *elles s'en payent une tranche*!

Are a lot of them undocumented?

Oh, they don't last long. It's impossible, in a neighborhood like this, you can't stay undocumented for more than five minutes, you'll be reported immediately by the other women, and then there's a whole network of balance, everyone's got to be in balance, more or less. Without meaning to, someone'll say, "Look, a new girl!" And then if you've got a cop out of uniform sitting at the next table, in the same bar, well, he pricks up his ears, and five minutes later people'll know the new girl's name, her age, how long she's been here, people will know everything, and then she will have to get the hell out pretty fast. Because the women are not going to tolerate an undocumented girl. Not on their lives; it means illegal competition for them.

Why illegal?

Because an undocumented girl's not gonna pay taxes, and she can break the prices, she can do all kinds of things.

So it's, like, a labor union.

There is a certain kind of regulation that's more or less implied: when you reach a certain age, you're not gonna take clients below the price, you are not gonna take them without a condom, you are not gonna keep them too long, I mean… this kind of regulation is tacit, an understanding. An eighteen-year-old girl, if she's starting to do clients at forty Swiss francs, fifty Swiss francs, sixty Swiss francs, the old ladies of sixty and more, what are they gonna do?

Nothing. You see, there is a hierarchy. Back in the day, I would have never done a client for fifty Swiss francs, that just didn't exist. But now I do it a lot, because I'll be fifty-two in a month. And when I'm seventy, well! Then maybe I'll do them for thirty francs, for twenty francs. I don't know. I don't even know if I'll still be here, but you see, age plays an enormous role.

Would you do them for nothing?

Not on your life!

But this whole business with condoms, what's it about? You never do that?

Yeah, sure, sometimes I put one on, when I can. Look, a lot of times the guys in the street ask me, "You do it with or without?" So I say, it's up to you, I give myself a little chance with them, but I've already understood that there isn't any. I mean, if I said, "Oh no! I always do it with protection.—Oh, well, let me think about it, or, I have to go park my car." And then you don't see them again, because obviously, they see a young girl of twenty right next to me who will give them the same answer, "Oh, with me it's never without," and they go to her, she's wearing tiny shorts, tall shiny boots, lovely thighs, a perfect little ass, a beautiful smooth face, they won't hesitate. But if you say, look, it's whatever you want, they think about it, they say look, there are five little twenty-year-olds who all said it would cost me a hundred francs with condom. But here's one who's a lot older, sure, but she'll do me without a condom, and I know she'll take good care of me, and maybe she'll even give me a twenty franc discount, so let's get on with it, no need to hesitate. You can easily see what's going on in their head. I can't allow myself the same demands as a gorgeous young woman of eighteen or thirty. You have to be reasonable.

And blacks, are there a lot of them?

There are probably undocumented ones… Ladies who come here as dancers or tourists, or secretaries, and who want to make a little cash at the end of the month. I adore the undocumented women, because I was undocumented myself, for years and years. I almost died of it. You had to stick to the walls, not talk to anybody, you had to pretend nothing was going on, and then I had my kids sleeping in some tent, I had the cops on my ass, the girls watching me, it was awful. So when I see a woman, furtive, who seems like she's suffering, hiding, I give her a little encouraging smile and I show her with my eyes that I won't betray her, quite the opposite, that I'm gonna help her.

Do a lot of people kick them out?

Oh, they run to the police station, they call, look, there's a new girl, she's not signed up, she's not declared, *quelle horreur*! She's taking our clients. And she's younger than us. You've got to see it, the women are ferocious!

Do the girls ever get pregnant? With a client?

Oh, well, there's one little girl, I don't wanna say her name because she'd rip my eyes out, she got pregnant with an Asian client, she has a wonderful little baby, a girl. She's a young woman who likes women, she's a lesbian. She'd never want to live with a man, or get married, she didn't want a father for her child at all. She wanted to have, as she says, a progenitor. She just wanted to make a baby. So she chose an Asian client, a Japanese guy she thought was cute, agreeable, clean, in good health, and she made herself a baby, and the client still has no idea.

He hasn't seen her since?

Never! She'd worked it out with her cycle, so that it would fall on a fertile day, and she did the client as usual, he paid her, but she didn't put the condom on him. She was pregnant immediately. She was lucky.

Would you be ashamed to have an orgasm with a client?

Not at all! You know, two nights ago, I saw one of my nice clients, who makes me come. I ran in to him at the bar right over there. I've gone out two or three nights in a row lately, because nobody's been coming around. You have to do at least one every two or three days, or you can't survive. So I ran into this man at the Aiglon [Eaglet] bar. We were listening to music, there are always musicians with their accordions, it's wonderful. I was at the bar, he came and sat down next to me. So we winked at each other.

You knew him?

We knew each other very well, yes. He's the one who looks a little like Cocteau. He's a great artist of the female orgasm. And I've told him, they should give you the Légion d'honneur for orgasms. So he pretended to be a little shocked, but he adores when I tell him things like that. He's very happy about it, because he isn't so young anymore.

Oh really?

He's a man of great distinction. He's certainly very cultivated, but it's mysterious. We don't know, with these men, who they're married to, why they have to go to whores sometimes, we don't know anything about them. So this one likes me a lot. At the bar, we were pretending to insult each other a little. Or not to know each other. But it's a game. We know each other very well. We're enchanted to meet again but we don't want to show it, you understand. So he says to me, "It's been a long time since I last saw you," meaning, also, what the fuck are you doing here? I have to run into you again! As though it annoyed him, but he's actually enchanted. And then we made a scene in public, even though we both know that in five minutes we'll be at my place on the bed. It's funny, huh? And he says to me, I should come out here more often, because I only come once every three months. I say yes, it would be better for your health, certainly. We joke around like this, with irony. And then he goes, well, in any case, I get the most pleasure at your place, so… He says that as though it's some kind of regret. As though it's in spite of himself. But in reality, he likes me a lot. So afterwards, he gets up the courage to stand up, to cross the bistro with me, to walk up all the sidewalks till he gets here, publicly. That's courage, after all. Because to display yourself with a hooker on your arm is pretty noble, I think. It's showing, well voilà, I chose her, and I'm going to her place. And everybody knows perfectly well he's paying. They know us too well. So he gets here, and I'm not in love with this man, it's impossible, since we only see each other every three months or every six months, so I can't be in love with a man I never see, who has a separate life from mine, who certainly lives with his wife, who maybe has children, I don't have any idea what he does with his life.

But each time you see him again, you have a little weakness for him?

But he pays me. He gives me a hundred francs. I don't do him any favors. I let him make me come, that's already not bad, but he's so good at it that it would be a crime against nature and against myself not to let him do it.

You don't feel wrong about it?

Listen, I work hard so that he has as much pleasure as I do! It's giving, giving. I don't neglect him. I give him excellent caresses, it lasts a long time. Only him, he'd get off faster than I would, so after a while he says to me, "Now leave me be, I'm going to take care of you." So I simper a little, I say ok, only if I want it, huh! But I know very well that I want it. I can't do otherwise, what do you want from me! I have nobody, I don't have a lover right now, not for a long time, so you have to let yourself go once in a while for your health, otherwise you become hysterical, we'd all be in the asylum if we never got to come, we need to be touched, to mess around, to be penetrated, to do this and that, we would go insane, because you always have to block yourself, restrain yourself, forbid yourself from coming, I mean, it would be ridiculous.

How many clients does this happen with?

Very few. There used to be a few who made me come, but now I don't let them anymore, because it unnerves me… I select the best ones. There are maybe two or three, and still… Sometimes I don't let them. I tell them no, no, today I'm tired… I find a pretext, I say no, it's not working. Today I'm gonna take care of you, but me, you just leave me be. So they obey.

Why do you do that?

Well when you're not in love, you know! It kind of… it makes you sad. Of course, with the body, you have a lot of pleasure, but… you don't have pleasure in your feelings, there just isn't love. It really can be terrible when there isn't love. So look, the gentleman I'm telling you about, he had caressed me admirably, licked me, he did everything there was to do, but he doesn't make me come by penetrating me, he makes me come on the outside, like this with his mouth, fingers, hands, and afterward he said, was it good? I said it was sublime. And it was true. I'm not lying, it lasted almost an hour. If I had been in love, it might have lasted ten minutes. But look, you have to make yourself imagine you're in love when you aren't, that's already almost exhausting. You imagine someone who doesn't exist...

Do you think of someone in particular?

Oh! I've often thought of the Berber, but there's no point in thinking of him anymore, he doesn't deserve it. No, in the end, maybe I think of no one. An imaginary lover who doesn't exist, voilà.

You called Tunisia this morning?

Yes, because all the same it's been a year and eighteen days or twenty days, I don't know anymore, since I had any news from the Berber.

A year?

Yes. This letter is dated 14 July 1980.

And he wrote on the envelope: Grisélidis Réal Ahmed...

Oh, my god! Because we were always pretending to be married. You know that when I met him he was in prison?

Yes, you've told me.

Right, and for a year and two months we'd been writing to each other, and I would go to see him every two weeks, it was a great love story.

And you just called him?

I called a place in Sidi Bou Said where he used to work sometimes in the summers, in a little restaurant. And yesterday, all of a sudden, first I took this letter out, and I saw 14 July 1980, so then I felt some anguish, because more than a year without any news… He could be dead, or in jail, or maybe happy, married, or maybe he's found… because he likes men too, he doesn't only like women…

And what did he say?

So wait, I make the call, and I hear a young voice with an Arab accent. I, right away, to situate things, so that it doesn't take too long, I said, I'm calling from Switzerland, I'm a friend of Hassen, that's not his real name, it's his brother's name. You know, these little gigolos always have fake names because of the cops and all that. He had been a gigolo for a long time, through his youth. In Saint-Germain-des-Prés, in Pigalle, all over. He had fake names and he changed them all the time. So I said, look, I'm a friend of his from Switzerland. And I could tell the young man didn't really understand. So I said, Where is Hassen? And there was a kind of excruciating silence. I said, fine, he's dead. And then he said, "Hassen? Ah! Hassen, he is not here.—But isn't he working this summer?—No, no, no.—So where is he?—In the souks." Ah, I finally exhaled. He's in the souks. So he's getting shitfaced, but that doesn't matter. I said yes, I'm a friend from Switzerland, so then there was another silence with a different quality, and the young man, you won't guess what he let out. He said to me, You're his wife? So then I was the one who didn't answer right away. *(Laughter.)* And then I said yes, yes. "You are Grisélidis?" I said yes, that's right. Can you imagine, in Sidi Bou Said, in the sand…

In the sand, yes.

He said to me, don't worry, we'll let him know as soon as possible. I said, listen, it's been more than a year that I haven't had any news from him, so even if he's angry, it doesn't matter, but he should write me a little card all the same, because I'm very worried. And then I added: is he happy? Then I felt a little uncomfortable, and then he told me no. But you don't know if they tell you that stuff so you'll send them cash or if they really are unhappy, I don't know. If he had really been miserable he would get shitfaced full time and would call me collect, dead drunk, at midnight. So he must not be as miserable as all that, especially not in the summer. There are tourists, there are caresses, wild beaches, cash, in the summer there's everything you need. It's in the winter that things go badly over there.

And what did he write to you the last time?

Well, look. 14 July, 1980, "To my love… You know, I am not angry that you have not written. I am used to the fact that you don't speak to me anymore." Yes, you know, we fight all the time! "I love you, Kitten, and I'm the one who is writing you because your love and your soul are haunting me…"

"Kitten"?

Yes, he calls me that… "And your soul is haunting me and killing me piece by piece. What does it matter to you. You're mad at me because of our fights. Love, know that in every love and union, there are always highs and lows. That's because of the violence of our unique weapon that is love. Verlaine shot Rimbaud with a revolver…" You see what I mean! So I can expect anything! "… and Oscar Wilde was ruined for Douglas, to be loved." He wrote loved, *aimée*, in the feminine, it's extraordinary. "I don't know how, unfortunately, to explain everything in writing, wrong (*faute*) as I am, too lost (*perdue*)..." Here too, he wrote "perdue" [in the feminine]... "in our feelings for you. Our love..." underlined twice... "so beautiful and unique, it is not your fault if this unique love is lost, it's my fault." At least he's honest here!... *(Laughter.)* "and I don't think you will come for me one day, anymore, because you're no longer the same. Forgive me for saying this to you, you have changed, because you will no longer speak to me..." Yes, but there are reasons! "your only love!" ... "Basically, the telephone is a comfort to me when I love you too much among the others. You have your place of physical lack. But inside me, you have always existed and you still exist, unique, unique, my female. Do not think that this letter is a letter of reproach. No, it's love, ours, that isolates me with you, even though you are so far from me, you are my one and only. I have fucked and assfucked and talked and drunk and drugged. I have given myself all the human drama and still, you are in me, I call you and I cry on the telephone..." Yes, that's true, and then afterwards he forgets to hang up, you should see my bills! *(Laughter.)* "... and I cry on the telephone and I have a soul that cries in sorrow to be separated from you. You are still concerned with an action that I have finished by no longer thinking about it and that has only separated us and wasted those few sentiments in us that we will never find in other people. We understood and loved each other, without even seeing or knowing each other. Yes, kitten, everything between us has changed, unique. Two bodies forever disunited, but my soul is in you forever"... Yeah, he repeats himself a little here! *(Laughter.)* "I will never forgive you for this waste, this desertion, this abandon of us. You've left me in the abyss, in solitude, in misery..." That's harsh, huh?... "No letters from you, you don't realize what that represents, a letter from you, when I finally receive it. My love, I am not dead, but many things in me are dead and sad, unhappy for me. Only you, my gypsy, artist, poet, my wife, my only love…" Oh, he's repeating himself… "I write you when madness enchants me…" Lovely turn of phrase!… "I love you when I want to hate you. I want you when I want to loathe you, I adore you when I want to leave you…" That's pretty extraordinary. Sometimes there are passages… "Beloved, I love you, Grisélidis, I'm speaking a little bit of myself to you, I'm at the beach as always, I'm not dying of hunger, I don't care about it. I'm managing. I get caresses from the burning sun, and I think of you, Kitten, I don't want to work anymore because it doesn't interest me anymore. I met my poet writer friend. We decided to record a book together soon, he talked to me about important things that I didn't know about them. And also he encouraged me. Everything is good for me… If I agree not to drink during work, because now there is a big house and space so that one can be at ease. He said to me, if your wife comes, you can live with her here, at his house. I answered that it would maybe be in a dream that she would visit me… But she doesn't give importance to life anymore, and also she's neurotic now that she's over fifty…" What nerve! *(Laughter.)* Bastard! It's unbelievable! "to show that she's in love…" Right, with what! "… and to sacrifice herself…" Oh, yeah right! "… or to give herself to me younger…" No, he's got stamina! "That is what I've understood of you, because to be busy all the time, I don't believe it. You are often sad and depressed the way I know you are, or else you have a lover. Bravo, Kitten! Live and fuck! One day, I will have happiness too maybe. Kitten, I love you. My only, Your man who adores you, Hassine." What a bastard! Because I'm older than him! Can you believe this!

It's a beautiful letter.

It's extraordinary. Well, I have a trunk full of letters, and he has two suitcases from me. Two suitcases! Because, when he was in jail, we made a point to write each other every day. Every day. And sometimes there were three letters a day! So it's possible that he could call me collect or write to me... Or maybe he won't write to me... Maybe he's angry for good. But that would surprise me. So this young man on the phone ended up saying to me: "He's my uncle!" Over there, they're all uncles, cousins, brothers, they've got enormous families, these Berbers!...

Who's the oldest whore in the neighborhood?

Well, there's one they call the Baroness or The Princess or The Countess, she's always saying that she's gonna retire. Year after year, she says, alright, it's my last year, I'm going to retire, and she's still here. So listen, she says that she's fifty. If she's fifty then I'm twelve! She must be getting near seventy, if not a little more, but I don't want to be mean. And furthermore, it's of no importance. She's still incredibly attractive. Like a grand empress.

Do some of them get plastic surgery?

Oh, I know a woman of sixty-four, she told me she was gonna get a face lift, and I said, are you sure you need to do that? You don't really need it. She said, yes, yes, yes I do, I'll be much better off. She has a younger lover. This is a totally balanced woman, she has her little life very well-organized, she has her clients, for years and years... At sixty-four... You have to have a faithful clientele to count on. This is a woman of extraordinary charm. She has a few wrinkles...

What about you, would you do that?

I would do anything to stay myself as long as possible. And if I really started to get too shabby, too ugly, too old, and if I wanted to please a man I loved, well! I'd do it. Why not? If it wasn't too expensive. But it's always a little bothersome screwing around with nature, don't you think? Because you see the faces of old men that are just splendor, you see photos of old Indian women, Eskimo women who are magnificent, with wrinkles, old. They are superb. So to recycle onself into a faux young woman… I don't know. I think there must be a malaise that would go with it. You wouldn't really be yourself.

But does a prostitute always have the air of a faux young woman?

But listen, I have photos of gypsy artists in their makeup on album covers, and they're great beauties! They are old, and they are made up like artists. They are not made up like faux young women, they are not made up like whores, but it's the same thing, because whores are often made up like gypsy women, why not? Or like Russian or Polish countesses.

And you, do you make yourself up like an artist?

I make myself up as myself, yes. Which is to say, as a gypsy artist. To please myself. Right now, I've totally reconnected with myself, one could say. Because I do go out in the street. Obviously right now I am not wearing makeup, as you can see. But when I am made up the way I am everyday, whether as a whore or just as a civilian, it's exactly the same. I haven't gone to the hairdresser in years, so I cut my own hair, I do my own makeup, and I dress myself as I am. It does happen that I go out dressed like this and I bring a client back, like this, as a regular person.

Wearing that skirt?

Certainly, and it's full of holes and patches, worn at every end, people find it wonderful. It's an old Indian skirt that has lived so much, it'll be in rags soon, even though I repaired it... Oh! My God, here's a new hole! I repaired it myself. Can you see all of these? They're old skirts from gypsies who walk barefoot in the forest, so they should never die, skirts like this. They'll croak with me. I want to be buried in an old skirt full of holes that has lived as much as I have.

How many clients have you had in your life?

Oh, thousands, thousands. I haven't counted. Everything I did in Germany, you know! Everything I'm doing again now... '77 to '81, it's been four years, but you realize at least a little all that we do! You can't count. There are immense armies that have passed over us. Waves and oceans of men who have passed over us, forests of cocks that have screwed us. It's marvelous! *(Laughter.)*

And the Moldy Rhinoceros? What's that guy all about?

Oh, he's an enormous Spaniard. In two years, he's gotten even fatter. You know, it's getting impossible. Soon he won't be able to get through the door. His stomach is so fat that he can't see his own cock, and besides, he doesn't have a cock. He doesn't have one. Have you ever seen a man without a cock? And you know, I don't know what's inside his stomach, I don't know if it's beer or despair, but he has a stomach... like this! I swear to you. He has such a sad gaze, it's so wretched, so so wretched, to such a point of misery, of solitude, that I just can't refuse him.

How old is this man?

It's undefinable. Just try and figure it out! Thirty, forty. Impossible to say. Despair has no age. He has no cock. In the first place, it's incredibly hard to wash it, I can't manage to really wash it because it's completely enclosed in the skin. And also, the balls are pretty fat, but not as fat as his stomach. So afterward, you bring him in front of the mirror, and you have to make something come out at all costs, it's hard! I'm buried under his stomach. He's like a Falstaff, he stands here like this! And I'm here, I'm choking, I can't breathe, I can't see anything, although there's nothing to see. So I manage to make a tiny bit of cock after, I don't know, twenty minutes of relentless effort! And he's wheezing! He goes like this! Hhhhhh! hhh! You keep thinking he's gonna collapse! And he always stands around for hours over there, in the street, contemplating my windows, it drives me crazy!

I am sure that you would have success in the windows. Like Roselyne, you know, she stands in her window naked, and there are armies before her... Everything, drunks, voyeurs, wankers who will finish themselves off after. So she says that they're all there, their heads turned. And her, when you see her breasts from below, she is more beautiful.

Let me tell you that right away, in five minutes, there would be a truck full of cops at the door and I would be packed off to Bel-Air, to the mental hospital. You can't do that around here.

Nobody does it?

This isn't Pigalle or Les Halles! No way! You can't do that. Right away, the old ladies across the street will call the police. It's impossible. They'd make you pay a fine for disturbing the public! *(Laughter.)* It disturbs public order and morality. So you have a fine to pay and on top of that they send you to the asylum to cure you, because you're not normal if you do things like that. Here in Calvin land, you can't do that, you can't show yourself naked!

What about the Auroch? The prehistoric beast?

He came back the other day. If you saw him in the street, I think you'd be a little afraid.

What does he look like?

Another enormous Spaniard, a beast, with a very tender side to him. He has balls as fat as this! Let me show you. Oh! Even this orange isn't fat enough. I didn't see them right away because he hides them a little, you see, but in the end I saw them, quelle horreur! They're like melons. It's an affliction!

Does he come often?

Oh, thank God he does not come often. I would be dead already, or in the asylum…

Why, is he brutal?

He is brutal because he doesn't come, it's always the same story. He never, never manages to ejaculate in a woman. So to finish it off, you see, it becomes prehistoric scenes. Because it unnerves him. It's neither my fault nor his. So he grabs me, and he practically tears me apart, I mean, he gets half crazy with nerves, this poor man, he masturbates savagely, I barely have time to take out a couple of Kleenex before it splatters on the ceiling and everywhere. It's an abomination. I get sick when I see it. And in the street, he greets me politely, he asks me how my children are doing, he's a simple, lovely man. He's made me some beautiful declarations in Spanish, while crushing me under his weight and grinding me to bits. He asks me if I want to be his wife, if I want to have his child. One would ask oneself how, poor thing. In Kleenex! But it's dramatic, you know.

Are there others who greet you?

Listen, you meet little groups of Spaniards at the end of the week, taking the air on a café terrace, or who are just talking to each other like they do in Spain, and they burst out laughing, some of them sing songs. So when they see you passing, since they're all your clients, they greet you with a smile. "How you doing? Good evening!" And then, sometimes, one'll slide into your ear, "You free?" or something like that. But there's no embarrassment, you see. We belong to them. It's family. I think it's beautiful, the simplicity of these men. They see a woman passing and they're accustomed to going to her at the end of the week, there's no problem.

Some have asked you to dance to a piece of music...

Oh, well yeah. Nothing is as obnoxious as that.

Dancing naked?

Oh la la, it never ends. Because you have to dance and dance, it lengthens the half hour. There was an old wino who always asked for that. In the end nobody wanted to do it, we were all sick of it. I mean, he wanted to dance with you. So he was glued to you... Covered in sweat, reeking of alcohol. With the red hairs under his armpits, nothing smells as bad as that! It was unbearable.

There aren't any Arabs who ask for that, Turks or Spaniards?

Oh, there are Arabs who come over, I always put music on. So they take their clothes off while dancing. They don't bother you. They dance by themselves. Like this… Look, they take their pants off, they take their shirt off, it's wonderful. They have dance in their blood. And then there are Spaniards who'll take you in their arms and do a little waltz or tango, but that's just friendly, it's not to be obnoxious. And it's not even sexual, it's just joie de vivre. For love of music and dance. For them, I think love, dance, and the body of a woman are linked. I mean, you know that Spain has the best dancers. It's a religion, dance, for them!

You've never done couples?

I did that once, because I was invited in private, but it didn't work very well. It worked for the gentleman, but the young woman complained that she didn't come. It was kind of my fault. Because since it was the only time in my life that I did that, I felt a little uncomfortable and I realized later that I hadn't done what I should have done. I was a little buzzed. We'd been drinking champagne, we'd celebrated a little, they'd prepared a beautiful table with a feast, champagne, alcohol, everything you can think of. I drank a lot. And I should have made sure to give this young woman pleasure, as I had been paid to do, but I didn't dare.

Was it a long time ago?

Yes! Yes, it was years ago. They invited me to their house in France, an HLM [rent-controlled housing] in Annemasse. Funny, huh? And the children were asleep in the next room. They were a real couple. Married.

You never did it again?

No, it's never come up. Once, I was at the house of a gentleman and a lady. I don't think they were quite a real couple, he was a very strange man, kind of a pimp. I was totally drunk... To show you how drunk I was, I was dancing naked except for a white fur! And after, with the woman, we were kissing, I mean, we were totally drunk. And I even felt pleasure. It was the only time in my life. And the guy came and put a lid on it and ruined everything.

What did Cannelle tell you on the subject?

Cannelle takes couples, and one can imagine that couples would want a little distraction, something with a mixed-race woman, but, in the end, it's not really about that. It's usually the pretext for a breakup. Because according to this young woman, almost all the couples broke up afterwards. And that means it was the pretext for the breakup. You understand, a three-way to demonstrate that things weren't working anymore. That the couple was finished. It's even happened that she'd see the woman alone, afterward, and she'd say, "Look, it's all over with my guy. And I prefer women anyway, I want to liberate myself." It's very curious.

And young married couples?

I got a call to consult with a pastor, once, I don't want to say his name because I don't want to cause him any problems.

Did this happen long ago?

It must have been two years ago I think, three years, I don't know. I was paid a lot of money. It was a young man who was about to get married, but he didn't know anything, so I had to make drawings to show him how to do it!

The pastor was getting married?

No, not at all. It was one of the young men he took care of.

He couldn't show him himself?

No. It had to be a woman courtesan, an expert, to explain it. So, I never made love with this young man, he was going to be married, and he did not want to make love with me, he wanted to make love with his wife, he just didn't know how to go about it. First there was a feast, a splendid meal, they paid me a lot, it was an act of generosity on the part of the pastor, I figured, because he never should have paid me so much. I was a little uncomfortable, but...

How much? Five hundred Swiss francs?

Yes.

And how long did the lesson last?

The whole evening.

And you only showed him pictures.

Not at all, had to talk, had to explain the mechanism of the female body, how to lubricate a woman, not to penetrate her like a beast, how to make her feel confident, how to show desire, I mean, I had to try to make as many barriers and taboos fall as I could so that their wedding night wouldn't be ruined, you understand. This young man had no experience, and he was in anguish. He needed a woman to talk to him. Of course you know that in families, nobody talks about anything.

How old was he, this boy?

He was kind of a choirboy, a very pure young man. A little bit of an ingenue, a little timid. He smiled a lot. We'd had a lot to drink, all of us were half in the vapors, and there were excellent bottles of Bordeaux, in that restaurant you eat and drink so well!

It must have been a rich family for the pastor to worry like that.

I don't know. Or maybe they'd all gone in together to help him pass the hat. I didn't ask questions. I did my best to instruct this young man in the company of a number of grand people, everyone was laughing, everyone was listening. But it was very thoughtful. They weren't making fun of him.

Was his wife there too?

Oh, certainly not!

There were only boys there, they were celebrating...

... his bachelor life. In the end, he was smiling, reassured, everyone applauded, they thanked me for my teaching, they told me that I'd pulled it off brilliantly, and to him they said, look, if you let yourself flunk your wedding night, we're gonna be angry. After everything she told you...

You never saw him again?

No.

And what's the story with the hunchback? He was a bit of a masochist?

Oh, you know, the story of the hunchback, that's a moving story. He wasn't masochist at all. He was a little dwarf. Listen. I was at home. Doorbell rings. It was nighttime. I open up and I see this tiny dwarf. I didn't see the hump right away, it was kind of hidden behind his head. He comes in right away. I saw the profile. It was like a camel. A hump, listen, like this! Yes! You're laughing! But... Only on one side of the back, on the right. Like the Pulcinellos you see on old engravings. Exactly like them. And it was real.

How old was he?

Oh, he must have been between thirty and forty. I was taken aback, you see. But you can't say, "No way, get out of here!"... That would be monstrously cruel, and it's just not done. So I said, come in, come in! I mean, I could barely breathe... So he sat down over there where you are, and then he might have been a little bit uncomfortable, because these are people who must suffer atrociously. He had a normal head, a normal body, but much too small, and this enormous hump, this enormous hump...

Well?

Well look, we discussed the price, and I didn't know—in addition to the hump, he might have been a poor laborer. That's not written on their faces or on their humps. He had a little bit of an accent, slightly foreign, but I understood afterward that it was a Swiss-German accent and I'd been mistaken. He said, how much does it come to. I said, fifty francs. That's the price for immigrant laborers, although later, you'll see that he added a little to that, but at the beginning, he gave me fifty francs. So I went to put it in my bag in the kitchen, as I always do. I came back here, he was already half undressed, but he'd left on what they call a little *liquette*, you know, a little workshirt, and the hump was under it, apparently. I said to myself, My God, on the one hand, it would be better if he didn't take that off because it will scare me too much and on the other hand, if he has enough confidence in me and in himself, he'll take it off, but I don't say a thing. I don't say a thing. I lit the candles, I took out the sheets, I unfolded them, I put the cushions around, I did exactly as I always do. I said, alright, we're gonna go bathe, and at that moment, he grabbed hold of his shirt and took it off. Then, you know, frankly, it gave me a horrible shock. I managed not to show it, but myopic as I am, that hump, you just saw it too much. That was all you could see in the room. Only on one side of the back, you understand!

And?

Well, I took him into the bathroom, he had a normal cock. I washed his cock, soaped it, rinsed, dried, and then we came back over to the bed, but then there was a problem, because I always say, you know, make yourself comfortable, put your head on the cushions, I tell them to lie down on the bed and then I have to do the preparatory things, I have to suck, caress, sometimes assfuck them a little with a finger, it depends on the situation. So he got on the bed on his side, like this, and I said to myself, I can't really suck him that well when he's on his side, because his thighs are in the way. And I saw that I'd have some work to do to get him into a good position. But by then, I was in a panic. And all of a sudden, I don't know how, it was as though the hump had been crushed, that it had gone back inside of his back or into the bed, I didn't really understand, and he lay down on his back, but with a terrible grimace. Can you see what I'm talking about! So I sucked his cock for a long time, I talked to him gently, and you know, I asked him his name, his name was Béat, that means "happy" in Latin. So this poor boy, not only did he have an enormous hump fatter than he was, but on top of that his name was Happy. Too much!

And why did you complain?

But wait! Because all the same, I had to work a lot, it took a very long time. And afterwards, well, he wanted to get on me, and I said to myself, I have to have the courage to treat him as though he's completely normal. I always rub their backs because it reassures them, and it's nice, you know, they make love better when you rub their backs. An Italian told me that, years ago, he said to me, when you pass your hand or your nails over my back a little while I'm making love, well, it works a lot better. So I did put my hand on his back, I touched that hump, and you know, it's as if the spinal column had been entirely deviated toward the right, and bent like the arch of a bridge, and pretty hard. I felt the vertebrae, so there were two columns, one on the back that wasn't visible and the other one forming the hump, or did he have one spinal column that was completely swerved, and swollen, I have no idea, but it's frightening to live with a hump like that.

They say it's good luck to touch a hump…

Oh, I don't know about that. I caressed it out of kindness, not curiosity, because on the one hand I was terrified, but out of kindness, in order to really show that I didn't want to treat him any differently. And then in the end, I felt a certain friendliness with this being, you see, even compassion, because you can't stay indifferent, first of all, the same thing could have easily happened to me.

And how did it end?

Well, he ejaculated normally when he was on top of me, fine, and afterward I went to bathe him and I said: you know, next time, you could give me twenty more francs, because I do a good job, don't you think? Which is to say, it really took a long time. So he was in complete agreement. He added twenty francs right there... Afterwards, I bathed, and while I was bathing, they're supposed to come back in here to get dressed. So I bathed, I dried myself off, I came back to make the bed a little, and he was lying down on it in fetal position. Like this...

Completely folded in on himself?

Yes. He was here, attached to the bed. I said, Well, what are you up to? He said, Ah! I'm staying here. You know, I could have cried. What he was saying was, I am so happy. I feel so good. I am staying here, right? I said, It's not possible. It's not possible, I have to work, but I could have cried. I said to myself, My God, he might actually be happy. Of course he wanted to stay here, in the warmth of a woman. It was atrocious of me to throw him out into the street, but what am I supposed to do? You can't.

You said to me once, It's the ones who have difficulty who come to see me, otherwise they'd go see the younger girls.

Of course.

Why? Because you have more patience?

Because the young ones, yeah, they kick them the fuck out the door in no time. If they see that a man has had too much to drink, or if he doesn't get hard in ten minutes, they say to them, "Listen, it's gonna be a hundred francs, or else you're out of here." But us, we can't do that, you see, women of my age. We have understanding and anyway, these men, they come here because they have a hard time, they need help. You can't throw them out, it would be inhuman. And then, they would never come back... You know, when you called me the other day, there had been that bomb at the station, placed by some Armenians, well, a funny thing happened to me then.

What happened to you? Did you jump?

Not at all. I went to the station to see the damage, but you couldn't see anything, there were police barriers, and afterward I went home, and it was raining, there was a terrible storm, I went home, and then a guy I didn't know came by. A tall blond young man. I took him, what do you expect, it's nice to have clients who come to my place, even if I don't know them in advance. This young man was practically impotent. He was in a horribly nervous state. Very tan, with thick muscular thighs, a beast, really a beast. Kind of Nordic beast. So, I'd tried everything, I put a finger in his anus, I sucked, I caressed, I scratched, I tried all the positions, he didn't get hard, I said, this one really has problems. He behaved a little bit like a child, he fidgeted a lot. He rubbed his thighs against each other the way a kid would do in bed, he masturbated, I mean, we tried everything. And in the end, he did come, but it had been very very taxing. And his aggressivity fell from the moment he ejaculated, so he was much more comfortable with himself, he started smiling again, became relaxed, friendly, and while I was bathing on my bidet, he read the articles that are up on the wall, and he said, Wow, you're interested in a lot of things, and every-thing. So I said yes, I'm making the revolution. He came up to me and then he said, "With the Armenians?" I said, Sweet Jesus! Maybe he's the one who planted the bomb! So you know, I didn't move. I stayed stoic, I said, oh, I make the revolution with all races, all countries, but peacefully, I said. Peacefully. But I didn't insist too much on that either. He was smiling, and he lit up, "Oh, with the Armenians?" Oh, I said, *quelle horreur*! That was all I needed. It's the guy who planted that bomb. He came to let off steam at my place, and on top of that, obviously, he's impotent. I mean, I am convinced that these terrorists are guys who have sexual problems. It's too flagrant! They have to get themselves going one way or another. You know, all the joys you can't have in a positive way, you try to have them negatively. I think that's a law of nature. I know a woman who used to be a sadomasochist. She got herself going by patiently getting tortured, beaten, whipped, wounded, cut with a razor, she even had to go to the hospital sometimes, she was so covered in deep wounds, burns, cuts, scratches, everything you can think of, and ultimately, she came to the end of her masochism. I mean, she just couldn't go on like that, because it wasn't working anymore, she had dulled herself. And now... now, she manages to make people snuff it, apparently, with black magic.

When clients cheat on you with another girl, does it affect you? When they go to someone else's place?

They don't cheat on me.

Does it sting you a little?

It keeps the jizz in circulation!

You say to yourself, oh, he's full of himself! I won't take him anymore, it's over!

You talk like a Calvinist! And you absolutely aren't one. When I see him with someone else, I say look, the little flirt, she must be pretty good at what she does, and pleasant enough, and he's doing the right thing.

And you make a little reflection on it for him about it when he comes back?

No. Nothing. There's no reflection to make. When he comes back, I say shit, him again!

Envoi

You know, I have to tell you again. My mother died ten years ago. We didn't get along at all, unfortunately. What's more, she arranged to die on my birthday, which was also my father's birthday. A triple date. So, the other day, when I had my fifty-second, I realized it had been ten years. I said, I should get up my courage and go see where she is. What's left. Two girlfriends of mine brought me by car to the Yverdon cemetery. And we looked through the tombs and didn't find anything. In the end, the gardener gave us a hand, and I saw something pretty extraordinary. You know my mother had an old girlfriend her own age, and I thought she must have been dead too, because the tomb looked completely abandoned. But since then, I called some of the old lady friends of my mother who were still alive, they told me that they'd had a granite plaque put on. Well, they're not as old as all that, they're my sisters. And I'd taken it for slate. You know why? Because it was totally cracked, that granite plaque. And in a crack there was even a missing piece, and there was a tuft of red flowers coming out of it. Like a dare, yes. Fantastic! She's still managing to say shit from the other side. And with flowers. Not bad, huh. I thought this woman had guts. And class. She was an artist. And she had gypsy blood like me.

2

LITTLE BLACK BOOK

There is nothing sweeter than thick Black lips. You rest your mouth on them, like silken cushions, they taste like cinnamon and nutmeg, they are magnificently blue-hued and tender. You can bite them without fear of wounding them. Their flesh is like mushroom, elastic and peppery, wet and refreshing.

— Grisélidis Réal, *Black is a Color*

Aymé (Boulanger) yeux
bleus, physique de catcheur-
~~Très~~ gentil- aime la douceur
et les caresses, longtemps-
a acheté "La Partagée"
A pris goût à un doigt dans le cul très peu à peu
Adrien énormes couilles
(hernie?) se branler, doigt
dans le cul, sucer partout
(pouah!...) 80 fs.
① André petit, sec, grisonnant-
enculer, sucer, baise-
dur à la détente- (lunettes) 100 fs-
Alec Petit homme doux
et tourmenté, ancien mili-
taire repenti, éjac-précoce-
60 fs-
Alfredo Sicilien presque nain,
sucer, baise, ne pas brusquer
70 fs. (Voir aussi à Fred)

A
B
C
D
E
F
G
H
J
K
L
M
N

AYMÉ (baker) blue eyes, catcher's physique, very nice—likes sweetness and caresses at length—bought *La Partagée*—Has developed a taste for a very tender finger in the ass.

ADRIEN enormous balls (hernia?) masturbates, finger in ass, suck all over (pouah!...) 80 F.

ANDRÉ short, dry, going grey—assfuck, suck, fuck—instantly hard (glasses) 100 F.

ALEC short little man, sweet and tormented, remorseful ex-military, premature ejac. 60 F.

ALFREDO Near-dwarf Sicilian—suck, fuck, do not rush him 70 F. (See also Fred.)

ALEX deaf, short, face a bit hard—no erection—manipulate with tenderness and an extreme care 80 F. Do not suck—fucks more or less...

1 ALBERT glasses, black beard, not much hair left, looks rather Presbyterian—professorial in a psychiatric way, apart from this gentle, cultivated, spiritual, dying to be fucked in the ass but doesn't dare (virgin anus very tight)—suck, fuck (fairly soft) 100 F.

2 ANDRÉ intellectual revolutionary, charming and intelligent, middle-aged, assfuck with tact and moderation, suck—fuck tenderly 100F. (Can give less when he's broke)—Particularly congenial man.

2 ALBERT M. nice man, corpulent—suck with art and delicacy 100 F. (Looks like a cop or civil service.)

1 ANTOINE artist (swarthy) like a well-behaved child—likes to be sucked with enthusiasm and dexterity—nice 80 F. (See his friend Gaston the fisherman.)

3 (?) ANDRÉ from Chamonix, looks like Bourvil—blond, a bit sentimental, sweet—suck with delicacy—finger near the ass—try to enter? Ejaculates in mouth 80 F.

ALAIN thin, swarthy, owns a snake ring exactly like mine—big cock, very contractile ass, suck, assfuck, fuck in duc d'Aumale position 80 F.

2 ANTOINE looks like an industrial peasant kind of down at heel, timid, sensitive—a bit bereft of hair—retired admiral jacket—extremely voluble prostate with arterial throbbing—assfuck with nuances while flattering the interior, while mouthing and cajoling the balls—at the end press and assfuck rhythmically while deepthroating—ejaculation in mouth 80 F.

AUGUSTO slightly German accent—nervous but nice, suck, lick, gets sucked until the end without assfucking, loud final moans 100 F.

ALI (from Yverdon) very nice, fat, not very tall, likes to take his time—hug, suck, assfuck, fuck—with conversation 150 F. (His wife has no understanding of fantasies.)

ANTONIO Italian, dark beauty ephebe look, dressed in leather, tight pants—mustache, curly hair—(looks kind of gangster/gigolo) likes to be dominated, insulted, assfucked, beaten, slapped—came standing in front of the mirror getting his cock sucked his balls strangled by a dog leash after having been whipped 100 F minimum.

1 BERNARD very nice, very sweet—silver-grey hair, suck and fuck normally 80 F.

BILLAL (?) nice Arab middle-aged very fat long cock, fuck à la Daddy-Mommy 60 F.

2 BERNARD gallant, country boy, age 58, very sweet, suck—fuck 80 F.

BASILE sent by Chantal suck, fuck 80 F.

3 BERNARD blond good kid, age 43, lives with his old stepfather of 70 who annoys him—(the one who killed my poor little cat)—suck, fuck 100 F.

4 BERNARD client from 8 years ago! A little bald, very talkative, funny—suck, assfuck, then fuck at doggie style 100 F.

BRUNO (from Neuchatel) (fiancé separated from his fiancée) blond, intellectual from the country, fuck, suck, tender and talkative 80 F. (Well-endowed.)

5 BERNARD from 10 years ago! slight Swiss-German accent, very brown eyes, fetishist—put women's lingerie on him, talk, coddle him, suck, assfuck, masturbates from 130 to 150 F.

THE STUTTERER fat man stutters horribly, looks slightly retarded, brought by Joseph (Italian with earring)—fat soft cock, rushes at me to embrace me violently all over—goes soft and doesn't ejaculate, horribly awful. 70 F says it'll take him 1 hour to make love (ask him for more). *Quelle horreur*!!

CHARLIE fat bearded guy tiny red beard, big dark yellow car, finger in the ass—nice, business in Frankfurt 80 F.

1 CLÉMENT age 64, thin, very brown body—(old mother's in a home, former prostitute), suck and fuck normally—comes in mouth 70 F.

1 CLAUDE age 20, locomotive conductor—blue eyes, little mustache. Very nice, "force of nature" physique, suck, fuck 80 to 100 F. (Sometimes more for 2 X.)

CHRISTIAN fat man, from the country, retired, has only one top tooth—nice, suck, fuck 70 F.

2 CLAUDE redhead, middle-aged—curly hair, very refined, kind, cultivated—(like a lawyer or intellectual)—sweet—suck, fuck 100 F.

1 CHARLES French, lives in the country, nice, sweet, normal 150 French F—suck, fuck.

2 CHARLES (sent by Josy) invites out to dinner—intelligent, kind, middle-aged, assfuck a little, prostate very deep—suck, fuck (condom) 100 F.

3 CLAUDE very strong Swiss German accent—going grey—pretty fat, brown eyes—suck with a lot of nuances, gently assfuck, prostate way inside 80 F. (Gave him the "Sexe fort.")

2 CLÉMENT former client from the old city, slim, tall, distinguished, crowned with hair, blue eyes—suck, fuck (condom) 100 F.

3 The great CHARLES big sensitive beast—going grey (former mental patient) lick the tips of nipples, suck, assfuck very gently without going too deep, comes in mouth 100 F.

4 CLAUDE fat cop-type beast, a bit aggressive, suck, fuck—capricious—comes in mouth 70 F.

CONSTANTINO Spanish laborer—short, old, slow and difficult hard-on—finger in ass, suck, fucks with difficulty—go up to 100 F.

5 CLAUDE middle-aged—fairly scientific intellectual—puts on airs (rapid ejaculator) fat cock horribly leaky—suck (especially the

balls)—embrace 100 F. (Offered him 2 X for 150 F.) (To console him for having come too fast in his hand while he was embracing me!)

6 CLAUDE Nice fat man, very tender, met near home on a rainy evening on way back from eating at L'Aiglon (The Eaglet)— French origin—suck, fuck 100 F. (Leant him *Pourriture de psychiatrie* and *La Redresse*.)

2 CHRISTIAN young (around 40) with a brown beard, black hair, muscular! assfuck, suck, fuck 100 F.

3 CHRISTIAN (from Berne) nice, forties, curly white hair, pretty chubby, suck in front of the mirror, then on the bed, deep assfuck, deep throat, 100 F. Interior of the anus fairly lamelliferous, buried prostate.

1 DANIEL met him one night around 1 in the morning, rue des Pâquis—bald, glasses, ugly face—comes in mouth, finger in ass, very taxing 80 F.

2 DANIEL young, nice, good-looking boy, suck, fuck—travels often—150 French F.

DOMINIQUE middle-aged, but young—Occasional musician (piano)—deflowered his ass (enchanted) comes in mouth 80 F.

DOUDOU weird Jew, wears stockings—makes Bible commentary—fuck at high speed 150 F.

3 DANIEL blue eyes, curly blond hair, stiff little cock, suck, embrace, came, me seated on him *par-derrière*—80 F.

DAVID fat middle-aged man—nice, slight Vaud accent, suck, assfuck a little, fuck 100 F.

DONATO Italian, looks like a labor boss, old handsome still vigorous, friendly, suck, fuck 80 to 100 F.

1 DÉDÉ going grey pretty bald salt and pepper, rimless glasses, cabinetmaker (?) (shows up one night with woodchips in his sandals!) strong, always thinks he's making me come (even just rubbing my breasts!) suck deep a lot of trembling for show 80 F.

2 DÉDÉ industrial peasant look, fat, going grey, blue eyes, has warts all over even under his cock… friendly, talkative, cuddly—suck, fuck 100 F.

ERIC very short, fat—likes bodysuits—nice, Genevan accent—suck, embrace, fuck normally 80 F. (Assfuck a little.)

EMILIO all clear—Very curly hair, medium height. Met at the top of rue Thalgerg—Genevan accent (age 50?) finger in ass, comes in mouth 70 F.

EDOUARD-LA-DOUCEUR, formerly butcher of Villette—Suck, fuck (if he hasn't drunk too much) finger in ass, masturbates 100 F.

EMILE very nice, suck, fuck 80 F (his wife doesn't know how to kiss).

1 EUGÈNE (Zurich) suck, fuck, 80 F (looks like The Suicide).

EDDIE ash blond, tall kind of captain look, looks like Eddie Constantine—deep throat with the proper nuances 100 F.

2 EUGÈNE (Yverdon) short, fat, glasses—very nice, bon vivant, from 100 to 200 F—likes to drink a glass of red and get assfucked by a big plastic electric cock (that he gave me).

1 FREDDY kind of Swiss-German accent, going grey, half bald, very nice—suck, put on a condom at the end—smooches—100 F. (Do NOT assfuck.)

2 FREDDY cultivated man, travels a lot—married his nurse—very very long—(gave me 500 F) talk, cajole—nuances to explore (a little finger in the ass).

FRÉDÉRIC nice tall young man, handsome, chestnut hair—likes sexy lingerie—suck, fuck (also high speed) deflowered his ass (?) 80 F.

FRANCO from Lausanne—nice Italian man fat cock vigorous going grey—suck, fuck 80 F.

FRANCIS nice Swiss-German—suck, fuck (widow) 80 F.

FRANCO (François) nice working-class Italian (missing teeth) fat balls—suck deep with lots of nuances 70 F (assfuck with movement).

3 FREDDY short man very nice, black hair, met one night in the old city—suck, fuck, with condom 100 F. Don't rush.

1 FRANÇOIS masochist filmmaker sent by Chantal—ties himself up with a rope—whip buttocks and upper thighs—suck—be in boots—long visual intellectual ceremony 200 F.

2 FRANÇOIS slim young man, intellectual look, a bit timid—suck, fuck à la Daddy-Mommy from 80 to 100 F.

3 FRANÇOIS corpulent Brazilian, short, a little bald—nice, likes to be sucked and cajoled, at length, in sweetness and music—suck 80 F.

FRED very short and bearded, suck, fuck, 70 F (sent by Tania). (See also Alfredo.)

1 GÉRARD tall dry going grey, met rue de Monthoux one Saturday late afternoon—suck, fuck, high heels 80 F.

1 GEORGES tall man, blue eyes, white hair, suck, ejaculates in mouth 100 F.

GUY Black from Madagascar extremely intelligent, friendly, likes well-done blowjobs (prostate like a flower) 100 F.

1 GILBERT enormous, age 45—suck, fuck me on top 70 F.

2 GILBERT works for Coca-Cola, silver-grey hair cut short, very chic, nice—suck, assfuck a little bit, slowly—fuck 80 F.

2 GEORGES nice fat wears glasses—little cock, suck, fuck 70 F.

3 GEORGES mustache, blue eyes, young, suck, fuck 80 F.

2 GÉRARD bearded curly hair pretty tubby, suck, fuck 80 F (doesn't give more than 70…).

3 GILBERT short fat, nice, old school (knows Chantal and Odette) suck, fuck 80 F.

GABY fat mustache, nice, suck, fuck, 200 French F likes it slow.

GUSTAVE tall emaciated old man, trembles, bumbling (Russian or Burgundian accent?!), wants to be punished very severely (plays dirty schoolboy surprised by teacher)—flay, scratch, spit and piss on him, insult and threaten, humiliate without shame (neither comes nor fucks—self-described diabetic!) (in reality doubtless impotent) 100 F (what a miser…).

4 GILBERT (arrived sent by a friend) peasant look a bit loutish but sensitive, sparse white hair, assfuck vigorously comes in mouth 80 F. (Now he wants me to put two fingers in ! !) Afterwards he fucks normally, him on me… Price unchanged… (widow of 2 years, lives in the country).

4 GEORGES pretty fat, a bit bald, shining black eyes, doctor or intellectual style, sweet—suck, fuck 80 F.

GASTON tall chic man, kind of bald, blue eyes, in his fifties German accent—suck, assfuck with a certain moderation and a fair amount of savagery (when suitable)—fuck 80 F.

5 GEORGES strong Swiss-German accent—going grey, very resistant fat cock, suck, sucks, fuck 100 F.

3 GÉRARD (from Chamonix) French middle-aged fairly well preserved—very hairy on the shoulderblades, very smoochy, affected, cuddler—deep throat *without assfucking* with infinite nuances while squeezing the balls (erection pretty soft) 200 French F.

GÉRARD French, bearded blond air of false intellectual—excite him with expert maneuvers (in reality fairly simple) nice, suck, fuck 200 French F.

6 GEORGES short blond blue eyes (?) Obsessed with his ass and by the color black (knows Chantal)—be dressed *all in black*, assfuck vigorously, suck, spit in his face when he comes in mouth 100 F.

7 GEORGES Spanish garage owner, tall, hairy a bit brutal but nice, immense cock very hard—suck, fuck 70 F.

2 GABY client from 11 years ago, bearded, force of nature, suck, pinch nipples a little, fuck 100 F.

1 HENRY man with grey hair, extremely distinguished, subtle, intelligent—Cocteau type—likes sweet finesse—100 F. Consummate scientist of the female orgasm... Doctor?... Psychiatrist?... Judge?... Assfuck on occasion while sucking until the end accompanied with "Japanese fire ants."

2 HENRY corpulent, blue eyes, not much hair left, white hair, breathless voice, wound up, timid and cerebral, extremely cultivated and kind, reads a lot of Greek and Roman authors—talk, caress—fuck (condom) 80 F.

HUGO young man with chestnut mustache, enormous cock, anus vast and welcoming, suck, fuck 100 F.

HERBERT of a certain age—face of a killer—short, pretty corpulent, grey hair—German (Jewish?) Sadistic fantasies—likes to humiliate and torture—can't get enough of getting his nipples licked and sucked, body, balls, anus—strangles, hits, pinches, crushes—do not scream— in the end makes me vomit strangling me with his dick—discharges in mouth after an atrocious ritual—gives up to 200 F. What scum!

INNOCENTE (Italian, locksmith), nice, blue eyes, pretty chubby, suck, fuck 70 F.

1 JOSEPH lives near the airport—Wife deceased two years ago— short, gallant—Do not rush—suck, fuck 70 F.

JAMES client of 7 years—Fat playful age 35—beautiful brown eyes, sailboat, talks a lot—suck, fuck normally (long) between 80 and 100 F.

1 JEAN slim, blue eyes, sparse blond hair—black suit magistrate or lawyer-type—stockings, garters—suck at length comes fast 100 F.

2 JEAN enormous, around 60, jacks off, discharges in mouth after a lot of trouble—walks with 1 cane 100 F.

1 JEAN-PIERRE going grey, extremely magistrate looking—nice voice —likes "leather"—suck, assfuck, finish with normal fucking 100 F.

3 JEAN client of seven years, enormous, distinguished gangster-from-the-Midi type, suck, finger in his ass, comes in mouth 100 F.

2 JOSEPH old Swiss-German—suck well and handjob 80 F.

JACKY (pastry chef) nice tidy man, likes to be sucked and caressed at length, suck, finger in ass, ejaculates in mouth, gave me 150 F.

4 JEAN sent by Chantal nice solid redhead, distinguished, beautiful cock healthy and vigorous—suck, finger in ass a little, tremble, pretend to come 100 F.

JEAN-LOUIS fat young man peasant footballer type—suck, fuck, do NOT assfuck—slow to finish but nice 100 F.

JEAN-LUC handsome mysterious young man, well-dressed—suck, fuck 100 F.

JEAN-FRANÇOIS nice boy athletic pale blue eyes—deep throat 100 F.

JEAN, thin, bald, old bachelor type, knows Chantal—assfuck slowly, suck 100 F.

1 JACQUES nice Italian sent by Chantal, fat cock, exterior of the anus sensitive, suck, fuck 50 F (very quick).

2 JACQUES very cultivated man, slight Swiss-German accent, suck, fuck 100 F.

6 JEAN nice Frenchman, beard, glasses, going grey—premature ejac.—condom. Painter in Annemasse 80 F.

JACKY good fat, athletic, fuck, suck 100 F.

JEAN-CLAUDE short bearded guy friendly kind of comes off as a yachtsman, suck, fuck (condom) 100 F.

4 JEAN-PIERRE force of nature, blue eyes, going a bit grey, film editor, suck, fuck 100 F.

KILLY sweet boy, bald, enigmatic (French?) lives in the country—suck his *derrière*, suck, embrace, came from behind me sitting on him 100 F.

7 JEAN fat pale redhead, pretty short, bit of a fuckhead, assfuck, suck, fuck 80 F.

8 JEAN age 54, white hair, fat short cock, suck, fuck, 70 F. Sent by Odette—(assfuck on occasion).

3 JOSEPH Italian, short, curly hair very hairy, green eyes, suck, fuck, 70 F. (Has 1 big white sculpted horn good-luck charm around neck) does not give more than 50 F ever since I made a mistake…

9 JEAN piece of shit, sure of himself, can't get enough of imposing himself, suck, fuck, falsely sentimental, heavy—finally ejaculates after having held it to the maximum 80 F.

3 JACQUES—gorgeous Porsche—young, refined, friendly—athletic, sensitive—suck with infinite nuance—do not assfuck—accelerate movement at the end—ejaculates in mouth 100 F.

10 JEAN runner cyclist on his way home, enormous muscles under the balls, white hair, nice, a bit slow to finish—suck, fuck 80 F.

2 JEAN-PIERRE adorable man, very sweet, very slim, pretty young, suck, fuck 80 F.

3 JEAN-PIERRE little cop-type shit, pathetic cock, endless cuddling if you let him do it, but ejaculates fast, only gives 50 F. (!) (*a disgrace!*)

1 LOUIS greying hair, a bit bald, nice, likes to suffer a little, fairly virgin ass, comes in mouth 80 F. Sent by Chantal.

2 LOUIS short, never gets undressed (suspenders) suck, fuck—(old, nice but pretty taxing).

His friend CAMILLE—old, medium…

1 LÉO Frenchman of Spanish origin—curly very black hair—suck, fuck 70 F. Loaned him *La Partagée* (returned).

1 LÉON gentleman of middle age. distinguished with a good-boy air—suck fuck, kindness 100 F.

3 LOUIS fat, tall, very blue eyes, intelligent and cultivated, doctor-type—suck, fuck, tenderness 100 F (bought *Nous ne sommes pas nées p.*) (white hair).

4 LOUIS athletic, greying hair, blue eyes, has traveled a lot—suck, fuck—fat cock—high speed 80 F.

3 LÉO "The Gardner" hefty man (Cross of Lorraine tattooed on arm) simple but intelligent, loves nature, sentimental—reformed gangster type—suck, fuck from 80 to 100 F.

LAURENT Mysterious jazz musician, sweet-violent—likes to be assfucked at length, fairly lively and alert Japanese fire ants, fuck at high speed 100 F (magnificent blue eyes, pale, slim, dressed in black, a bit pierrot lunaire).

1 MICHEL (television) very nice, intelligent, normal (gave two books, *Recherches* and *Barbara*) 100 F.

1 MARCEL enormous guy, cock very short, *do not suck* comes very fast—let him suck pretending to come at penetration 70 F.

MANUEL Spanish, gets excited undressing the woman—suck—does not want to come in mouth—works at hosto 80 F.

MICKY huge car crepuscular, comes from London—suck, fuck—sentimental 100 F.

MARIO Italian mustache suck, fuck 80 F (assfuck at beginning).

2 MARCEL small sick old man—Very nice sent by Josy—stay on top of him squeezing vagina, pinch nipples, he must not come (by medical order?!) 100 F. Comes nevertheless sometimes.

2 MICHEL (sent by Josy) nice, sweet, bald—deep throat while carefully assfucking 100 F.

3 MICHEL (sent by Odette) tall slim, Simenon type with glasses, premature ejac., let him play and embellish 70 F.

MIKE enormous pig, cop type, brutal, ejaculates between breasts. 70 F (ask for more).

4 MARCEL not very tall, light eyes, military haircut, a bit brusque, even brutal—suck, fuck, talk to him, cuddle 100 F.

4 MICHEL black, student, tall, thin, wonderful eyes, enormous thick cock, suck as long as possible (to manage my vagina…) 60 F.

6 MARCEL fat boy with a mustache butcher boy type—nice, do *not* pull back the foreskin, caress the lower abdomen, and the upper thighs while sucking delicately—fuck Daddy-Mommy style 80 F.

7 MARCEL sweet man, erudite, going grey, blue eyes, nice fat cock—suck, fuck—talk, reads a lot (brought a bunch of documents) 100 F.

5 MICHEL the electrician—young man of 33 "force of nature," eyes light and sensitive, sentimental wanting to seem a little tough, egotistical—generous—has done bio-energy—astrology—suck, fuck (monumental cock, but soft) 80 F.

6 MICHEL sent by Odette—masochist restauranteur cultivated and sweet, glasses—likes to be dominated, assfucked, humiliated, beaten 100 F.

MAURICE psychiatrist, intelligent, handsome and kind. Masochist. Very hard erection; comes under torture. Deep assfuck; bite, scratch, pinch nipples, handjob, suck. 200 F and up. Trample on him a little. Very dark, not too tall. Black eyes and hair.

7 MICHEL very amiable bearded "yachtsman" type, blue eyes, back a bit ill (I sent him to Asian massage) age 45, suck, tenderness, fuck 100 F.

OSCAR tall Swiss-German—bald—buried eyes—huge awful cock—60 F *demand* more. 70 F if you beat him, and 100 if you piss in his face—insult and slap vigorously.

OTTO sparse hair—Swiss-German accent—sent by "Gilbert"… which one?!). Suck, assfuck carefully, jacks off at the end looking at my anus—gave me 130 F. (In error perhaps?…)

PEDRO hilarious fat Spaniard, devotional, simple, honest, fat peasant face, in his 50s or 60s 70 F.

PIERROT tall, slightly redheaded, blue eyes—suck, fuck—refers to my breasts as "roberts," from 100 to 150 F.

1 PIERRE (of the perfumes) Tall blond, suck, assfuck, comes in mouth 80 to 100 F.

2 PIERRE tall, thin, young—erection fairly soft—suck while assfucking with precaution—with condom 80 F. (Does not want to be assfucked anymore! !)

PHILIPPE musician, young, very handsome (also drives trains) magnificent hair, beautiful eyes, tall, slim—assfuck, comes in mouth 100 F.

3 PIERRE Austrian, mountain climbs, young, handsome, saw me on French TV—suck, fuck 100 F (comes in mouth, finger in ass, lower the price).

4 PIERRE (from Versoix) young, corpulent—suck, fuck. 70 to 80 F.

1 PAUL (from Lausanne) short dry sentimental (has a "habituée" in les Pâquis) suck, fuck, 70 F.

2 PAUL client of 7 years, around 50, nice, sentimental suck, fuck, 100 F (calls me Goddess of Love!).

5 PIERRE strong Swiss-German accent, from Zurich, tall thin, going grey, wants to bring me flowers—suck, fuck 100 F.

6 PIERRE (of the Museum) charming man, very sweet, a bit bald, had an accident—treat him with patience and attention 80 F.

7 PIERRE tall, force of nature, gigantic cock *enormous*, assfuck, suck—fucks pretty brutally (alas) with condom. 100 F (blond, blue eyes, little mustache, distinguished).

8 PIERRE (from Basel) blue eyes, fifties, a bit bald, cultivated, sweet-violent—likes to take his time, drink, smoke—innocent erotic fantasies, pinch and bite nipple tips very hard, suck, assfuck sometimes, licks my finger once removed from his anus, licks up his come after handjob—from 100 to 400 F. It sometimes happens that he fucks normally—says I have a "body à la Vélazquez"...

9 PIERRE tall redhead distinguished travels to Africa—big cock with an enormous head—suck, assfuck vigorously, very hard prostate 100 F.

10 MONSIEUR PIERRE—tall man fairly corpulent, married, tortoiseshell glasses, blue eyes, a few white airs left, traveling diplomat type, kind, sweet, suck, sucks, fuck 100 F.

11 PIERRE tall very thin, age 40, glasses, not much hair left—likes music and ecology—semi-intellectual Frenchman—comes in mouth—do *not* assfuck—suck with a great deal of art and nuance, Japanese fire ants, etc. 80 F (says I am a "parenthesis in Time").

PSYCHOLOGICAL CASES

1. G has never had sexual relations with women—(with older men—*active*) forties, sensitive, loving, cultivated—problem with his old mother—father dead (15 years of psychoanalysis).

2 sessions of approach, discussion, fondling—will explain himself to his mother on my advice—met a bisexual boyfriend with whom he has relations and who explains women to him, their sexuality.

3rd *session* gets hard and ejaculates after an hour of work in mouth, massage of prostate (completely loose and passive).

11. DANIEL has never made love with anyone. Light, then stronger erection on me—while looking at me—gently caress anus—create a soft, romantic climate (forbidden childhood loves).

After many sessions: erection sometimes very strong and long-lasting—sperm mounts and then goes back down... *never* ejaculates, forbids himself unconsciously, obeying a taboo produced by a very old culpability and by his fidelity to his mother and the surveillance exerted on him by her when he was a child when he desired her (Oedipal complex to eradicate). He needs to become conscious of this and overcome his fear and a certain form of cowardice that paralyzes him (fear of being *punished* and abandoned by his mother, fear that she will no longer love him, that she will prefer his father...) has also repressed a passive homosexuality (possibly also active) unconscious since adolescence, desiring to be penetrated by his father and perhaps to penetrate his brother, and vice versa, the mother being *taboo* and sexually frustrated herself, apparently, to *punish himself* for having desired his mother, to expiate his guilt, and at the same time to be penetrated himself in place of his mother in order to protect her, and to *avenge* her by taking pleasure in her position, while also avenging himself for all of the sexuality that had been forbidden him and that he had repressed. To be continued.

SPECIAL CASES

LE GROS ROBERT (FAT ROBERT)—*enormous* man, adorable, has been sick for years (the only one I allow to use my bidet)—(has already murdered, with his weight, a bed and armchair! !) Make sure that his ulcers are bandaged or closed (otherwise they're lakes of blood)—suck, talk, drink whisky (often brings it to me himself) (jacks off on occasion) 100 F. Do not rush him, stays up to an hour, very spiritual.

1 ROLAND fat and bald—likes conversation—suck, fuck 80 F.

1 ROGER white beard, short mustache that stings, likes to suck at length, comes fast 100 F.

1 RENÉ short blond, French, comes in mouth very simply, do not rush 70 F.

RICHARD accent slightly Swiss-German, short, brown, muscular—(waterskiing) 80 F (suck, fuck).

1 RODOLPHE going grey, not very tall, beautiful big car metallic blue—condom—suck a little, fucks from behind lying on side 80 F.

1 RAYMOND very short, bald—Jewish (?) suck, fuck—60 to 80 F?

2nd ROGER of a certain age, thinks he makes women come with a vibrator! from 60 to 80 F—suck, fuck.

2nd RAYMOND light Swiss-German accent—likes to be beaten, tied up, tortured, jacks off—suck, nipples 100 F.

ROME (car mechanic) short friendly fat—suck, normal fuck 70 F.

2 ROLAND very simple, rustic quick work (suck if possible to the end without seeming to go too fast) 60 F. ?

3 ROLAND heavy brute—suck, fuck—(building painter) 70 or 80 F.

3 RAYMOND handome young blond muscular, mysterious, maso, slave—assfuck, suck, fuck 100 F.

3rd ROGER suck—assfuck, comes immediately in mouth, 100 F (of a certain age, a bit bald, very polite).

RÉMY met at my old place, nice, likes normal love—caresses, etc. 100 F.

ROGER nice thin wears glasses, fat cock, easy—suck, fuck—80 F.

2 RODOLPHE fat, old, reeks of piss and shit, horribly slow—80 F (suck, handjob).

ROBERT French hair going grey a bit thin, mustache, *do not suck*, handjob while talking dirty, prepare Kleenex, lick buttocks a little—150 French F. (Was finished off on telephone by Jackie Huguette one night from Paris!)

5 ROGER (from Alexandrie) once a student of my father's—sweet, a bit timid, kind, cultivated and intelligent—suck, fuck, give him a friendly price (not less than 70 F).

6 ROGER dirty old man, bald, keeps his underpants on as long as possible, simpers, gropes, fuck 80 F.

2 RENÉ (the color orange) sweet man, kind, black hair—suck, fuck 80 F.

4 RAYMOND intellectual drunk type a bit rustic, nice, silty blue eyes, past his fifties—suck, fuck fairly slowly 80 F.

ROBY fat pig, wants bang for his buck—embrace, suck, do not unsheathe glans—screw 100 F.

4 ROLAND gallant man, mustache, walks with a cane (accident) suck at length with thorough assfucking 80 F.

3 RENÉ French, bald, cultivated, lives in the country and on a boat—fuck, assfuck (fairly virginal anus) had a gall-bladder operation 220 French F.

7 ROGER French, age 63—lives with a young woman who won't let him lick her pussy—very careful, suck, fuck—gave me 150 F.

RAPHAEL strong build, black hair, older, brown eyes—tiny cock that grows—suck, fuck, nice 80 F.

8 ROGER (sent by Odette) Lebanese not very tall, mustache and glasses, beautiful deep voice rolls r's, suck, assfuck artistically, prostate very lively and sociable, treat with moderation otherwise it goes too quickly 100 F (lower to 80).

5 ROLAND artist, publicist, charming, sentimental, chestnut hair (light eyes) suck, fuck 100 F.

1 SERGE Italian—suck, fuck him lying on the bed me straddling him ass facing him 50 F.

STAN fat hairy braggart—traveled to Egypt (poultry merchant) suck, fuck 80 F.

2 SERGE cultivated man, scientific and humane, fat and kind, looks like a big mysterious Buddha—deep throat with nuances *sans* assfucking 100 F.

SIMON sentimental—nice, likes to talk, caress, embrace, mustache, cap—night guard at the factory, suck, fuck 80 F.

3 SERGE, chauffeur—bodyguard to a foreign ambassador—slim man, charming, 3 years older than me, has traveled a lot—knows asian breathing methods and secrets—only likes to be sucked off, at length and very thoroughly with interminable nuances—*exterior anal* caresses (did not really like internal caress, even though prostate reacted violently at the end)—from 100 F.

TONIO Portuguese very simple, very nice—suck, fuck 80 F.

TONY athletic intellectual type, sweet not very tall, blue eyes—deep throat while assfucking delicately 80 F.

3 YVES tall mysterious young man, very light eyes, fixed pupils, trembles rather bizarrely, assfuck delicately and tenderly, finish with fucking in maternal position 100 F.

1 WALTER slender man, body of a Greek shepherd, looks extremely young will soon be 50. Sent by Chantal—Suck, fuck 100 F. Do NOT assfuck.

WILLIAM from Vaux a bit rustic, fat, kind—*assfuck*, suck 70 F.

WALTHER man going grey, distinguished, cultivated, wears glasses, light American-Belgian accent—suck (sixty-nine) 100 F.

3 WALTHER young Swiss-German man, very nice, travels a lot, works in disinfectant products—foreskin does not peel back—suck, fuck 80 F.

WILLY charming man Mediterranean type, very cuddly (romantic gangster or intellectual type) suck, sucks, assfuck slowly (or not?) 80 F. (Could almost be in love with him…) (Oh la la…!)

1 YVES musician especially wonderful—just makes love 100 F.

2 YVES (?) wears glasses, square head—normal, suck, fuck 80 F. Do not assfuck!